Contents

Royal Navy Yearbook 2022: Warships – Submarines – Helicopters – Roya___ ___arines

LEFT: A Royal Marines raiding force has a key role in Britain's new naval strategy. (MOD/CROWN COPYRIGHT)

FAR LEFT: The 1982 Falklands Conflict saw the Royal Navy deploy the bulk of its ships, submarines, and aircraft to the South Atlantic to defeat the Argentine forces occupying the islands. (ROYAL NAVY)

LEFT: The Royal Family has strong links to the nation's Navy and here Her Royal Highness The Princess Royal says goodbye to the submarines HMS *Talent* and HMS *Trenchant*. (MOD/CROWN COPYRIGHT)

Photo Credits
The editor has attempted where possible to credit the originators of all the images used in this publication. Any errors will be corrected in future editions.

Britain's naval power has received a major boost with the entry to service of the two Queen Elizabeth-class aircraft carriers. (MOD/CROWN COPYRIGHT)

Royal Navy patrol vessels have been in the news monitoring migrants crossing the English Channel and protecting fishing grounds in the Channel Islands. (MOD/CROWN COPYRIGHT)

ISBN: 978 1 80282 445 2
Editor: Tim Ripley
Senior editor, specials: Roger Mortimer
Email: roger.mortimer@keypublishing.com
Design: SJmagic DESIGN SERVICES, India
Cover: Dan Hilliard
Sub editing: Sheena Harvey
Advertising Sales Manager: Brodie Baxter
Email: brodie.baxter@keypublishing.com
Tel: 01780 755131

Advertising Production: Debi McGowan
Email: debi.mcgowan@keypublishing.com

SUBSCRIPTION/MAIL ORDER
Key Publishing Ltd, PO Box 300, Stamford, Lincs, PE9 1NA
Tel: 01780 480404
Subscriptions email: subs@keypublishing.com
Mail Order email: orders@keypublishing.com
Website: www.keypublishing.com/shop

PUBLISHING
Group CEO: Adrian Cox
Publisher, Books and Bookazines: Jonathan Jackson
Head of Marketing: Shaun Binnington
Published by
Key Publishing Ltd, PO Box 100, Stamford, Lincs, PE9 1XQ
Tel: 01780 755131
Website: www.keypublishing.com

PRINTING
Precision Colour Printing Ltd, Haldane, Halesfield 1, Telford, Shropshire. TF7 4QQ

DISTRIBUTION
Seymour Distribution Ltd, 2 Poultry Avenue, London, EC1A 9PU
Enquiries Line: 02074 294000.

Welcome

A New Navy for the 21st century

ABOVE: HMS *Defender* on patrol in the Arctic during NATO exercises in February 2022 as the Ukraine crisis escalated. (MOD/CROWN COPYRIGHT)

RIGHT: The Royal Navy was centre stage during the state funeral of HM The Queen on September 19 when 142 Naval Ratings pulled the State Funeral Gun Carriage bearing her coffin from Westminster Hall to Westminster Abbey. They then pulled the carriage from the abbey to Wellington Arch as part of the main funeral procession. (MOD/CROWN COPYRIGHT)

Welcome to the first edition of Key Publishing's *Royal Navy Yearbook*. This new annual publication aims to provide a wide readership with information on what Britain's naval service – the warships and submarines of the Royal Navy, the fighting troops of the Royal Marines and the support ships of the Royal Fleet Auxiliary – have been doing over the past year and its future direction, as well as looking back at its illustrious pedigree.

British naval power has a history that stretches back before the Norman Conquest in 1066. During the Tudor era, the English navy became a global force to be reckoned with after Sir Francis Drake's famous victory over the Spanish Amanda in 1588. Once England and Scotland were united, the fleets of the two nations combined to form the first British naval force, that was henceforth known as the Royal Navy. In 1755 the first Marine divisions under naval direct command were formed to take over from army regiments that had been formed to fight from ships in 1664.

One hundred years ago the Royal Navy emerged from World War One as the world's dominant naval force. Its supremacy was not just to do with having numerical advantages over every other nation's fleet. The Royal Navy was at the cutting edge of naval technology, fielding the first purpose-built aircraft carriers and combat-ready submarines.

This era of overwhelming naval supremacy did not last long, however, as Britain entered a series of economic crises in the 1920s and 1930s which resulted in major cuts to the operational fleet and the future ship building programme. By the start of World War Two, the Royal Navy could just about dominate the waters of the North Atlantic and Mediterranean, but the Japanese and Americans had elbowed British maritime power out of the Far East. The sinking by the Japanese of the battle cruisers HMS *Prince of Wales* and HMS *Repulse* off Singapore in December 1941 ended any illusion

that the Royal Navy was the world's sole naval superpower.

Today, the Royal Navy may not be a rival to the American, Russian, or Chinese navies in terms of numbers, but it is still the most powerful western European navy. It has two new aircraft carriers, an effective nuclear power attack submarine fleet and a potent amphibious landing capability. The Royal Navy is also custodian of Britain's nuclear deterrent.

Defence cuts in 2010 hit the Royal Navy hard and resulted in the early retirement of its Invincible-class aircraft carriers. This financial situation has now been reversed and a new wave of building warships and submarines will stabilise and then grow the size of the fleet over the coming decade.

Naval warfare does not stand still and future battles and wars will not be won

The outbreak of the largest war in Europe since World War Two has seen the Ukrainian and Russian armed forces locked in intense combat, including several major naval engagements. At the same time China has been flexing its naval muscles around Taiwan. These events have thrown up many lessons that the Royal Navy is taking on board and we look at the implications for British sea power.

We hope you find the *Royal Navy Yearbook 2022-23* an informative read and that it stimulates further interest in Britain's maritime forces as they move to keep ahead of the latest trends in naval warfare.

Tim Ripley
Editor
October 2022

ABOVE: The late Queen's funeral on September 19, 2022. The tradition of the 123-year-old gun carriage being pulled by a human team goes back to the funeral of Queen Victoria in 1901 when the carriage's horses bolted just before the funeral and sailors stepped in to perform the duty. (MOD/CROWN COPYRIGHT)

LEFT: Editor Tim Ripley on board HMS *Prince of Wales*. (TIM RIPLEY)

BELOW: Royal Marines prepare to launch a training exercise from RFA *Mounts Bay*. (MOD/CROWN COPYRIGHT)

by past reputations alone. So, today's Royal Navy is aiming to keep itself at the cutting edge of combat tactics and abreast with tomorrow's technology.

We start off our first edition of the *Royal Navy Yearbook* with the First Sea Lord and Chief of the Naval Staff, Admiral Sir Ben Key, explaining the challenges facing his service and its future plans.

In the following chapters we look back at several famous Royal Navy battles and campaigns to bring alive the experience and sacrifice of past generations of British sailors and marines. The 40th anniversary of the Falklands conflict has been marked this year and we examine the role played by the Royal Navy in this historic victory.

At the heart of the Royal Navy is its famous ships, submarines and aircraft and we look at them in some detail to provide a snapshot of their capabilities today.

Global Fleet: Global Role

The First Sea Lord, Admiral Sir Ben Key, looks at the crises and conflicts that are shaping current Royal Navy operations and its future strategy.

ABOVE: British carrier airpower is available to respond to global crises.
(MOD/CROWN COPYRIGHT)

RIGHT: Admiral Sir Ben Key has ambitious plans to grow the Royal Navy to allow it to project naval power on the global stage.
(MOD/CROWN COPYRIGHT)

In July, the Royal Navy's senior officer, Admiral Sir Ben Key, talked to the Council on Geostrategy at the Naval and Military Club in London on the challenges facing Britain's Naval Service.

"We find ourselves in a time when the geopolitical landscape is changing before our eyes," said Sir Ben. "We're seeing increased state-on-state tensions, and transnational issues like the pandemic and climate change which are driving us to adapt. The nature of the threats we are facing is changing and how we are responding as a government and as instruments of national power is also changing.

"In my last role as the Chief of Joint Operations, when I took over [in March 2019] the majority of our overseas international commitments, defence deployments, outside of those with NATO, we were in the Middle

Hosted by the IISS

FIRST SEA LORD'S SEA POWER CONFERENCE 2022

5 May 2022 | #sea...onference

East. By the time I handed over, in October of last year, we had virtually no one serving in Iraq and nobody in Afghanistan – what a profound and rapid change that was, the speed of 20 years, two decades worth, of commitments in the Middle East.

"In the maritime we're seeing ever-increasing movement: of people, goods, and data across and under the seas. Almost half our food and gas reach us by sea. 97% of global communications are transmitted by undersea cables. Global merchant shipping tonnage has almost quadrupled since 1990 as over 90% of the world's goods move by sea and increasing amounts of our power, domestic power, is being generated offshore.

"Now, as First Sea Lord, I have been charged by the Government to ensure the Royal Navy is the leading navy in Europe. Maritime is the key to unlocking the nation's potential as a global trading nation. This has been true for over 400 years, and probably many more, and will be so long into the future.

"My underlying message is this: focusing solely on the Russian Bear risks missing the tiger. The conflict in Ukraine offers a number of lessons for us: the first shows the interconnectedness across the global commons. Rising fuel prices, shortages of food staples and raw materials are all, in part, traceable to Russia's illegal invasion. By trying to choke Ukraine's access to the sea, Russia is restricting the Ukrainians' ability to trade and exercise their rights of free and ≫

BELOW: Kinzhal hypersonic missiles, which have been used in action during the Ukraine war, being launched from MiG-31 jets. (RUSSIAN MINISTRY OF DEFENCE)

ABOVE: The Chinese People's Liberation Army Navy launched its third aircraft carrier, the *Fujian* in June 2022, dramatically raising the stakes on the naval arms race in the Pacific region. (PLAN)

BELOW: The Chinese J-15 jet is a locally produced variant of the Soviet Su-33 supersonic fighter. (PLAN)

offer ships, submarines, Commando Forces operating intimately with the Army, and fifth-generation aircraft in a shared endeavour with the RAF as part of our commitment to NATO. And the ability to operate in the near and far abroad at the same time is the hallmark of our naval forces.

"For while we see Russia as the clear and present danger, China is posing the long-term challenge. According to the World Bank, China's gross domestic product is already ten times that of Russia's. Last year China spent $293 billion on defence, growing their defence budget for the 27th consecutive year, whilst Russia spent $66 billion – less than a quarter. All of us recognise China is a nation with big ambitions. From the Belt and Road Initiative to the String of Pearls, from 'island building' in the South China Sea to designs on Taiwan."

Sir Ben also quoted the *Wall Street Journal*, which reported in June: "First by stealth, then by degrees, and now by great leaps, China is building a blue water navy and a network of bases to extend its military and political influence."

He continued: "The same month [as the *WSJ* article] the People's Liberation Army Navy launched its third aircraft carrier, the *Fujian*.

open access. The world is being held to ransom by a maritime blockade. It is that stark. Putin has, through his actions, created a new Iron Curtain from the Baltic to the Black Sea.

"The reality for us in the Royal Navy, is that recent events haven't knocked us off course. We've been modernising and transforming the Royal Navy for the last three years; we've cut back on duplication, invested in automation, and freed up more people for the front line. We are a 'light footprint' Service with global reach. The Royal Navy has two roles: to protect the UK home base and also to promote our wider global interests and security. That means we shadow the foreign warships going through our waters and protect our undersea cables from hostile submarines. We

ABOVE: Projecting power ashore in complex operational scenarios is the job of the Royal Marines. (MOD/CROWN COPYRIGHT)

THE FIRST SEA LORD

Educated at Bromsgrove School, Worcestershire, Ben Key joined the Royal Navy in 1984 as a University Cadet, subsequently graduating in Physics from Royal Holloway, University of London. He qualified as both helicopter aircrew and as a Principal Warfare Officer.

He has commanded four ships: the mine hunter HMS *Sandown*, the frigates HMS *Iron Duke* and HMS *Lancaster*, and the aircraft carrier HMS *Illustrious*.

Shore appointments have included Head of Navy Resources and Plans and Principal Staff Officer to the Chief of Defence Staff in the MOD and as an advisor to the Iraqi Director Joint Staff in Baghdad. From April 2013 to July 2015, he was Flag Officer Sea Training, responsible for recruiting as well as individual and operational training across the Royal Navy.

Promoted to Vice Admiral in February 2016, he was the Royal Navy Fleet Commander from then until March 2019. He then served as the Chief of Joint Operations, prior to his appointment as First Sea Lord in November 2021.

Admiral Sir Ben Key. (MOD/CROWN COPYRIGHT)

This is the first Chinese carrier to rival a Nimitz-class in size and the first to shift from a ski ramp to electromagnetic catapults. We are seeing the Chinese develop perhaps the world's largest navy in terms of pure hull numbers, coupled with a massive Coastguard and maritime militia.

"So, as an instrument of national power, alongside the diplomatic and trade arms and our sister services, we in the Royal Navy must mirror this global reach, building partnerships and integrated capability with fellow maritime forces in the near and far abroad.

"Now this is grand ambition, exciting opportunities, a maritime moment. But you can rightly ask how we will realise it. What does the Integrated Review [of March 2021] and subsequent events in Europe actually mean?

"What it means is we find ourselves at a moment that none of my First Sea Lord predecessors have enjoyed since the end of the Second World War. We are charged to grow. We have a degree of change set upon the service, a scale of which proportionately we have not had for 18 years. First, we must deliver on the Government's really significant investment in our ambitious shipbuilding programme:

Type 31, Type 32 and Type 26 frigates, the future support shipping and, with the Dreadnought-class submarine, the new generation of continuous at-sea deterrents – all of which must be brought into service over the next 10 to 15 years without dropping a single operational fall. This is no piecemeal investment, but a real coordinated shipbuilding drive.

"We have our direction from [last year's] Integrated Review and the Defence Command Paper. And we face a range of increasing threats to respond to, and will shortly have a new national maritime security strategy that will further integrate us into the nation's peace and prosperity agenda.

"Our Service provides the first line of the national defence – our boats and our Marines and the last line, our Vanguard-class submarines moving deep, silent, and undetectable somewhere below the waves. So, standing here in my tenure as the First Sea Lord, a moment in a long, long history, I'm determined that we will strive to retain the trust of the nation, something hard earned over many centuries, that our dependence on the sea is being protected and enabled. We feel it in our bones, in every operation we undertake."

The Fleet in 2022

Royal Navy Operations

Britain's naval power in 2022 is deployed around the world to protect sovereign territory, UK interests and to support allies.

Royal Navy commanders have a range of warships, submarines, aircraft, and Royal Marines units they can call upon to fulfil operational missions. They constantly juggle the maintenance schedules of their vessels with operational requirements to ensure that naval force elements are available for routine tasking and to be mobilised in response to unforeseen events.

The Royal Navy today has a mix of main force elements – surface warships, submarines and aircraft that are capable of high-end warfare – and supporting units such as patrol craft and Royal Fleet Auxiliary ships that can be employed to support civil authorities, law enforcement

and border security and to provide humanitarian aid.

Main Force Elements

The most obvious symbols of British naval power are the two Queen Elizabeth-class aircraft carriers. They are both currently in service and the Royal Navy operates them on a readiness cycle, with one ship available for operations for a year at a time while the other undergoes scheduled maintenance. Last year HMS *Queen Elizabeth* led the Carrier Strike Group 21 deployment to the Far East and this year HMS *Prince of Wales* is taking part in active operations.

The core of the Royal Navy's warfighting capabilities is its destroyers and frigates. Its 12 Type 23 frigates are the most active surface warships and one is always held at high readiness in UK waters or at its home port ready to be scrambled in case of emergencies, such as escorting Russian warships through UK waters. Another Type 23 – currently HMS *Montrose* but soon to be replaced by HMS *Lancaster* – is forward-based in Bahrain in the Arabian Gulf to operate in the Middle East alongside the Royal

LEFT: The bridge crew of HMS *Queen Elizabeth* edge the 65,000-ton carrier out of Portsmouth harbour ahead of her historic mission to the Far East in 2021. She has had a quieter year in 2022. (MOD/CROWN COPYRIGHT)

Navy's forward-based mine counter-measures task group. Four or five Type 23s are usually in maintenance or overhaul, which leaves around five ships that are routinely available to support training exercises and NATO deployments or to protect the carriers when they deploy.

The next most important element of the surface fleet is the six Type 45 destroyers. However, they have often been plagued by technical problems with their electric drives and crew shortages. Over the past decade it has been common for three or four them to be tied up in Portsmouth at any point in time. The Type 45s are integral to the carrier strike groups and one is needed to accompany the aircraft carriers at all times during operational deployments in order to provide air defence cover. »

BELOW: The Royal Navy's submarines are on duty round the clock somewhere in the world, although their movements are closely guarded secrets. (MOD/CROWN COPYRIGHT)

RIGHT: RFA *Mounts Bay* was in the Thames to join the June 2022 celebrations of HM The Queen's Platinum Jubilee.
(MOD/CROWN COPYRIGHT)

BELOW: A Sea Viper missile is launched from HMS *Diamond* to demonstrate the air defence capabilities of the Royal Navy.
(MOD/CROWN COPYRIGHT)

The submarine force is central to the delivery of the UK's nuclear deterrent. One of the Vanguard submarines is always at sea, ready to respond to a nuclear threat against Britain. To sustain this continuous at-sea deterrent, the other Vanguard submarines, which are known in the Royal Navy as V-Boats, are locked into an intense cycle of training and maintenance to ensure that a new submarine is always ready and able to take over when a submarine finishes its deterrent patrol.

To support the V-Boats, attack submarines have a key role in patrolling the access points to the Clyde submarine base in Scotland as the Vanguard submarines are leaving or returning to port. They make sure that hostile submarines are not able to track and trail the British missile boats. When a V-Boat is on patrol, an attack submarine is routinely sent along to ensure no hostile submarines are nearby.

The four Astute class and one remaining Trafalgar class submarines, with their Tomahawk land attack missiles, have an important role to play in wider British defence operations. At least one attack boat must be available to sail at speed to provide an on-call missile strike capability if a crisis should develop anywhere in the world. The old Trafalgar boats were plagued by technical problems, though, and it was routine for only two or three of the seven boats to be ready for action at any point in time. With the new Astute boats availability has improved and by the middle of the decade the full seven submarines should be in service.

Getting fully equipped and trained warships sea ready for operations is a complex business that involves several months of training and exercises. Supporting helicopters and aircraft of the Fleet Air Arm, for example, are an integral part of Royal Navy warships and their crews need to train to embark on them.

The Royal Marines are also held at readiness to operate on Royal Navy warships, either as small-force protection and boarding teams or as larger amphibious landing forces. A battalion-sized Royal Marine Commando unit is on alert to embark on Royal Navy and Royal Fleet Auxiliary landing ships and provide an amphibious task group. Over the coming years, under the Future Commando Force concept, a company-sized unit of Royal Marines will be embarked permanently on landing ships. These are dubbed Littoral Strike Ships and they will be forward-deployed in the Gulf region and European waters.

A programme of deployment of Royal Marine training teams is now underway to provide military assistance to allied nations in Africa, the Middle East, and Eastern Europe.

Supporting Units

In addition to its main force elements, the Royal Navy also has standing commitments to operate in UK home waters and British overseas territories.

The protection of the UK's 200-mile exclusive economic zone has been a key Royal Navy task for several decades, with Royal Navy River or Archer-class patrol boats assigned to fishery protection duties. Other patrol boats are permanently based in Gibraltar and the Falklands. A patrol boat, or a Royal Fleet Auxiliary ship, is also permanently deployed to the Caribbean in the hurricane season to stand ready to provide humanitarian aid to British overseas territories in the region.

Task Organisation

The Royal Navy is a task-orientated organisation and it has a flexible command system to control a range of operations. Its Maritime Battle Staff, based at Navy Headquarters in Portsmouth, is a scalable organisation that can deploy either as a large two-star headquarters to command a major operation or be broken down into a number of one-star headquarters to control smaller operations of shorter duration.

The days of senior naval officers commanding battles from the bridge of a warship are well and truly over. The Royal Navy now controls its operations in a very flexible way using satellite links and other modern communications technology. Communications connectivity is the key to modern naval command, allowing commanders and their staff to access intelligence, such as video feeds from unmanned aerial vehicles or satellite imagery, in real time. Naval task groups are now connected by data links that allow radar returns to be merged instantaneously to create a common air or surface picture that can be viewed in the operations rooms of warships. In the modern era this is the equivalent of looking out from the ship's bridge and seeing the enemy fleet. This technology gives naval commanders a god's eye view of thousands of square miles of sea. Naval commanders in the 21st century have access to unprecedented amounts of information that their predecessors could never have imagined.

Britain's Naval Bases

Sustaining the Fleet

HM Naval Base Portsmouth: Home of the Fleet

BELOW: The Royal Navy's two new aircraft carriers are home ported at Portsmouth.
(ITOOKSOMEPHOTOS)

Portsmouth Naval Base has been an integral part of the city since 1194. It is home to almost two-thirds of the Royal Navy's surface ships, including the aircraft carriers HMS *Queen Elizabeth* and HMS *Prince Of Wales*, the Type 45 destroyers, several Type 23 frigates, as well as mine countermeasures and patrol vessel squadrons. The base is a major civilian employer and more than 7,000 naval personnel serve there or on Portsmouth-based ships. HMS *Victory*, Admiral Lord Nelson's famous flagship, is preserved in the dockyard and still serves as the First Sea Lord's Flagship.

HM Naval Base Devonport, Plymouth: Frigates, Landing Ships and Royal Marines

The largest naval base in Western Europe, Devonport has been supporting the Royal Navy since 1691. The vast site covers more than 650 acres and has 15 dry docks, four miles of waterfront, 25 tidal berths and five basins. The base employs 2,500 service personnel and civilians, supports around 400 local firms and generates around 10% of Plymouth's income. Devonport is home to Britain's amphibious ships, survey vessels and half the Royal Navy's frigates, plus the Flag Officer Sea Training organisation and the Royal Navy's Amphibious Centre at RM Tamar.

Also in Plymouth are several Royal Marine bases, including the headquarters of 3 Commando Brigade in Stonehouse Barracks. Across the River Tamar is the HMS *Raleigh* base where all naval recruits receive their basic training.

RIGHT: The Devonport Naval Base is home to the Royal Navy's amphibious forces and several frigates. Babcock run major warship and submarine overhaul facilities on the site.
(MOD/CROWN COPYRIGHT)

HM Naval Base Clyde: Submarine Hub

Faslane Naval Base is home to the Royal Navy's Submarine Service, including the nation's nuclear deterrent, and the new generation of Astute submarines, as well mine countermeasures and patrol vessels. The nearby Royal Naval Armaments Depot at Coulport is responsible for the storage, processing, maintenance, and issue of key elements of the UK's Trident missile system and the ammunition for all submarine-embarked weapons.

ABOVE: Britain's nuclear missiles and warheads are stored at RNAD Coulport, close to Faslane. (OFOG DIRECT AKTION FÖR FRED)

LEFT: The Faslane base is home to the Royal Navy's Vanguard and Astute-class nuclear submarines. (MOD/CROWN COPYRIGHT)

Culdrose and Yeovilton: Naval Air Stations

The Fleet Air Arm now has two main operating bases that house its fleet of helicopters. Royal Naval Air Station Culdrose, just outside Helston on the Lizard Peninsula – is one of the largest helicopter bases in Europe, being home to the Royal Navy's Merlin helicopters and unmanned aerial vehicles. With 3,000 personnel, HMS *Sea Hawk* is one of the biggest single-site employers in Cornwall.

RNAS Yeovilton is home to the Fleet Air Arm's Wildcat Force and the Commando Helicopter Force, plus vintage aircraft of the RN Historic Flight.

The base is located near HMS *Heron* in Somerset and covers around 1,400 acres with the main airfield in Yeovilton itself and the satellite at Merryfield. Some 4,300 personnel, service and civilian, including Ministry of Defence employees and permanent contractors, are employed on the site. The air station also hosts a large support staff from the Defence Equipment and Support organisation, and the Fleet Air Arm Museum.

There is a growing Royal Navy presence at RAF Marham in Norfolk,

LEFT: Royal Navy Wildcat helicopters are based at RNAS Yeovilton in Somerset. (MOD/CROWN COPYRIGHT)

where the F-35B Lightning jump jets are based.

Commanding the Fleet: Naval Headquarters

The Royal Navy is administered from the Naval Headquarters building on Whale Island in Portsmouth but it does not have operational command of its ships and submarines at sea.

Surface ships operating outside UK waters are usually directed from the Permanent Joint Headquarters in Northwood, London. The Royal

Navy's Commander Operations is also based at the Northwood site and its staff controls all naval operations in UK waters, as well as being responsible for the Commander Task Force (CTF) 311 that controls UK attack submarines, and CTF 345 that controls the UK nuclear missile submarines.

Also at Northwood is the NATO Allied Maritime Command which, when activated, controls NATO naval operations in European waters. It is commanded by a Royal Navy vice admiral.

Where is the Royal Navy?

Global Deployments

For centuries, the Royal Navy has sailed the seven seas, flying its famous White Ensign. The British Empire may be long gone but it is still true to say that the sun never sets on the Royal Navy.

In the summer of 2022, the global deployments of the Royal Navy give a snapshot of the service's typical daily activity.

For the early part of this year, the Royal Navy paced its operations to give a well-earned rest to the ships, aircraft and thousands of personnel who took part in the Carrier Strike Group 21 deployment to the Far East, led by HMS *Queen Elizabeth*.

Earlier in 2022, HMS *Prince of Wales* became the flagship of the naval element of NATO's Response Force, leading 35,000 personnel during Exercise Cold Response and demonstrating the UK's commitment and deterrence capability in the High North region. The Royal Navy planned to step up its activities in the autumn with a cruise by a naval task group led by the carrier HMS *Prince of Wales* to the east coast of the United States. However, the carrier sailed from Portsmouth on August 27 but suffered a technical fault a few hours later. She had to return to port for repairs and HMS *Queen Elizabeth* was ordered to take her place. It had been planned for HMS *Queen Elizabeth* to sail to join NATO exercises in the Baltic and Mediterranean later in the year, but these were put on hold.

Russia's invasion of Ukraine in February 2022 prompted a renewed focus by the Royal Navy on operations in European waters. Subsequently, several Royal Navy warships joined NATO exercises in the Mediterranean, Baltic, and Norwegian Seas to reassure allies and deter Russian aggression. The Royal Marines joined allied exercises in Norway, using equipment and supplies forward-based near the Arctic circle. For several months, hundreds of Royal Marines from 45

East. During 2022, two patrol craft, HMS *Tamar,* and HMS *Spey*, have been operating East of Suez as part of a five-year long mission.

The Royal Navy has responsibility to protect and support British Overseas territories and continues to provide ships and personnel to show the flag. In 2022 the patrol ship HMS *Forth* has sustained the naval presence in the South Atlantic and HMS *Medway* has cruised the Caribbean. HMS *Trent* has also supported the two patrol boat vessels of the Gibraltar Squadron.

Since January 2022, the Royal Navy has been supporting the UK Border Force operation to prevent migrants crossing the English Channel from France to Kent in small boats.

LEFT: The Royal Navy has joined the operation to prevent migrants crossing the English Channel to the British coast in small boats. (MOD/CROWNCOPYRIGHT)

Commando were on duty in Poland, helping to train the Polish and Ukrainian forces. Royal Marines Arctic warfare specialists also continue to support British Army units in the Baltic states, providing dedicated cold weather training to hundreds of soldiers each year.

The Royal Navy retains a strong presence in the Arabian Gulf and permanently bases four mine countermeasure vessels – HMSs *Middleton, Bangor, Chiddingfold* and *Penzance* – and a support ship, RFA *Lyme Bay*, at the UK Naval Support Facility (NSF) at Mina Salman Port in Bahrain. Since late 2018, a type 23 frigate, currently HMS *Montrose*, has also been forward-based in Bahrain to enhance Gulf security. Crews are UK-based and rotate every few months. Additional frigates and/ or destroyers can be deployed when necessary.

In addition, a new permanent Joint Logistics Support Base at Duqm Port in Oman opened in 2018. Both the enhanced NSF and Duqm will support the future deployments of the Queen Elizabeth-class aircraft

LEFT: Royal Navy surveillance experts are providing intelligence support to the Border Force as it tries to stem the flow of migrants across the English Channel. (MOD/CROWNCOPYRIGHT)

carriers, and Duqm also has a dry dock facility. The Ministry of Defence said Duqm gives the UK "a strategically important and permanent maritime base east of Suez, but outside of the Gulf".

A British Defence Support Unit is also based in Singapore to assist Royal Navy warships operating in the Far

Operation Isotrope involves the Royal Navy providing command and control assets, as well as occasional Batch 1 River- and Archer-class offshore patrol vessels and RIBs. By the beginning of August 2022 the Ministry of Defence had reported that 20,000 migrants had crossed the Channel compared to 11,300 by the same date in 2021.

BELOW: HMS *Lancaster* on exercise off Norway in 2021. She then headed to the Arabian Gulf for an extended deployment. (MOD/CROWNCOPYRIGHT)

Operation Pedestal 1942

Saving Malta

In the summer of 1942, British forces in North Africa were on the verge of defeat. German troops of the Afrika Korps were pushing towards the Suez Canal after capturing the Libyan port of Tobruk. All that was holding back the German advance was a lack of fuel, caused by British air and submarine attacks mounted from the island of Malta.

Situated at the centre of the Mediterranean, Malta was a constant thorn in the side of the Germans and their Italian allies. As a result, it was under a round-the-clock air attack and supply ships heading to the island were top targets. By August Malta's 300,000 population was on the verge of starvation and its military garrison had only a couple of weeks' of ammunition and fuel left. If the island could not be resupplied it would be forced to surrender.

Prime Minister Winston Churchill resolved that Malta could not be allowed to fall. He ordered the Royal Navy to mount Operation Pedestal to break the Axis blockade of the island. By early August, the largest fleet ever assembled by the Royal Navy in European waters in the war so far was gathering in Gibraltar ready to sail eastwards to Malta to escort 14 merchant vessels past rings of German U-boats, Italian battleships and torpedo boats, backed up by more than 500 Axis aircraft. From bases on Sardinia, Sicily and Pantelleria, the Axis forces could mount a relentless assault on the British convoy.

The British naval forces were comprised of three aircraft carriers, two battleships, seven light cruisers, 32 destroyers, four corvettes and four minesweepers. Air cover was limited to 74 fighters flying either from the carriers or out of Malta. A further 38 Spitfires were embarked on the aircraft ferry carrier, HMS *Furious*, but they were destined to reinforce Malta's battered air defences and were to be launched on a one-way mission to the island when she got within range. Naval chiefs told Churchill that losses would be heavy, but the Prime Minister ordered the operation to begin anyway.

Within hours of the fleet sailing from Gibraltar on August 10 it came under relentless attack by German and Italian submarines. One submarine got through the destroyer screen and

put four torpedoes into HMS *Eagle,* which went down in eight minutes. Although more than 900 of the aircraft carrier's 1,160 strong crew were rescued, all but four of her aircraft were lost – 20% of the fleet's air cover.

From then on the attacks were relentless. On August 12 and 13, as the convoy neared Sicily, four escorts were sunk or badly damaged. The swarms of Italian torpedo boats took aim at the vital merchant vessels, sinking four and damaging one.

Then the air attacks started to escalate. On August 11, 36 German bombers targeted the convoy. More came on August 12 with a massive wave of 72 German aircraft being launched at the British fleet in the morning. Later that day 120 German aircraft hit the convoy, leading to the loss of three merchant vessels and another three being badly damaged. Few of the surviving merchant ships and escort vessels were undamaged and their crews were traumatised by the unrelenting attacks.

By August 13 the convoy was within range of Malta's Spitfires and air attacks started to diminish. Three of the surviving merchant vessels made it to Malta later that day and another followed early on

August 14. One vessel, the severely damaged oil tanker SS *Ohio,* was still at sea being kept afloat by two destroyers and a minesweeper that were lashed to her hull. The vital tanker eventually limped into Valletta Harbour early on August

14 to cheering crowds of islanders. Her cargo of aviation fuel meant Malta's Spitfires could keep flying for several more weeks.

Operation Pedestal achieved its aims. The five merchant vessels delivered 32,000 tons of general cargo, together with petrol, oil fuel, kerosene, and diesel fuel. It was enough to give the island about ten more weeks of supplies. The price had been high, though. Thirteen vessels, including nine merchant vessels, one aircraft carrier, two cruisers, a destroyer, as well as 34 aircraft had been lost. Nearly 500 British sailors, both Royal Navy and Merchant Navy, lost their lives. As well as saving Malta from falling, Operation Pedestal proved to be the last major naval battle of World War Two fought entirely by the Royal Navy. For the remainder of the war Britain's Navy would operate in tandem with its new American allies.

ABOVE: Malta's Grand Harbour as seen from a German bomber. The heroic island was relentless pounded during the summer of 1942. (IWM)

LEFT: The oil tanker SS *Ohio* limps into Valletta's Grand Harbour in Malta. After she successfully off-loaded her cargo, the valiant ship sank. (IWM)

The Falklands Conflict 40 Years On

Royal Navy in Operation Corporate

ABOVE: The destruction of **HMS** *Sheffield* after she was hit by an Argentine Exocet missile shocked the nation and the Royal Navy task force in the South Atlantic.
(MOD/CROWN COPYRIGHT)

In March 1982 Argentine scrap metal merchants landed on the British Antarctic Territory of South Georgia. At the time the event received little attention, but the crisis soon escalated and by the end of the month an Argentine invasion fleet was sailing toward the capital of the Falkland Islands, Port Stanley.

As Britain's eavesdropping organisation, GHCQ, decoded signals traffic to the Argentine fleet ordering the invasion and occupation of the Falklands, Prime Minister Margaret Thatcher ordered a crisis meeting of her cabinet ministers and military chiefs to work out what to do.

On the evening of 31 March, Thatcher and her advisors gathered in an office in the House of Commons. Just by chance the senior British military officer in London was the head of the Royal Navy, Admiral Sir

RIGHT: Fleet Air Arm Sea Harrier fighters and RAF Harrier strike jets won the air war over the Falklands.
(MOD/CROWN COPYRIGHT)

FAR RIGHT: The Battle for the South Atlantic.
(US MILITARY ACADEMY)

Henry Leach. He made his way to the meeting in his full dress uniform, complete with medals and gold braid. Ministers and civil servants advised the Prime Minister that there was little that could be done to reclaim the Falklands. Thatcher turned to Leach and asked him if the islands could be recaptured. The First Sea Lord did not equivocate. The Royal Navy could and should be sent to the South Atlantic to restore British rule to the Falkland Islands, he declared. The rest, as they say, is history. Two days later, bolstered by Leach's robust response, Thatcher ordered a naval task force to the South Atlantic and, on June 14, the Argentine garrison on Port Stanley surrendered.

Over the next 100 days the Royal Navy fought its biggest and most intense naval campaign since World War Two. The Falklands Conflict was the Royal Navy's first experience of combat in the missile and electronic warfare era. It was also the first – and to date only – successful sinking of an enemy warship by a nuclear power attack submarine. That historic attack by HMS *Conqueror* on the Argentine cruiser the ARA *General Belgrano* on May 2 proved to be the decisive naval action of the war. It ensured the Royal Navy could operate around the Falkland Islands without interference from the Argentine Navy for the rest of the war.

To land the British assault force of Royal Marines, Paratroopers and other army units on the Falklands, the Royal Navy then only had to deal with the Argentine Air Force.

The formidable nature of the Argentine air threat became apparent on May 4 when the Type 42 air defence destroyer, HMS *Sheffield*, was hit and set on fire by a French-made Exocet sea-skimming guided missile. The destroyer's defences proved unable to detect the incoming missile until it was too late. Twenty sailors died and 26 were seriously injured after the missile hit. The attack left the nation in shock. It was the first major British warship to be lost to enemy action since World War Two but it was not to be the last. The Royal Navy lost four warships and several others were damaged. Hundreds of sailors had been killed or wounded on those ships by the time Port Stanley fell.

For the remainder of the campaign the task force commander, Rear Admiral Sandy Woodward, had to juggle his meagre force of Sea Harrier jump jets with the divergent requirement to protect his two aircraft carriers – HMS *Hermes* and HMS *Invincible* – and the amphibious shipping putting the land force ashore. The loss of the carriers risked putting the whole campaign in doubt, so the amphibious force had to take

its chances in 'bomb alley', as British sailors soon nicknamed San Carlos Water. There were just not enough Sea Harriers to fly combat air patrols over the Falklands and protect the carriers all the time. The Royal Navy's Sea Harriers operating around San >>

ABOVE: Rear Admiral Sandy Woodward was on-the-scene commander of Royal Navy forces in the South Atlantic. (MOD/CROWN COPYRIGHT)

LEFT: The carrier HMS *Hermes* was the vital base for British airpower in the South Atlantic during the Falklands war. (MOD/CROWN COPYRIGHT)

Carlos proved to be effective killers of Argentine aircraft, but they did not have the range to patrol off the West coast of the Falklands to intercept enemy aircraft as they approached the islands. They could only intercept the Argentine jets after they had dropped their bombs and were heading for home.

The amphibious landing at San Carlos on the May 21 achieved total surprise, catching the Argentine command unawares and the bulk of the assault troops were safely ashore before the enemy knew what was happening. So, by the time massed Argentine air attacks started, most of the troop transport ships were empty. The job of defending the bridgehead and anchorage fell to the Type 21 and Type 22 frigates assigned to the amphibious task group. Argentine jets gave the frigates a real pounding in San Carlos Water, sinking two and

RIGHT: **HMS** *Conqueror* was the first – and to date only – nuclear power attack submarine ever to sink an enemy warship.
(ROYAL NAVY)

ABOVE: HMS *Invincible* returned home from the South Atlantic to a hero's welcome at Portsmouth. (MOD/CROWN COPYRIGHT)

severely damaging two others. But Admiral Woodward knew that if the Argentines were bombing his frigates they could not also be attacking the vital amphibious shipping or the troops ashore. The Battle of San Carlos Water proved just as decisive as the sinking of the ARA *General Belgrano*. The Argentine Air Force inflicted heavy losses on the Royal Navy, but the landing was not interrupted.

Once ashore, the Royal Marines of 3 Commando Brigade led the advance under the command of Brigadier Julian Thompson. The Royal Marines of 45 Commando were the vanguard of the drive on the capital of the Falklands. There were not enough helicopters to move all the troops and their equipment so 45 Commando picked up their Bergen rucksacks and marched across mountains and bogs to Port Stanley. By the first week of June the ground forces, then under the command of

Royal Marine Major General Jeremy Moore, were positioned in the hills above Port Stanley ready to strike. Royal Marines attacked and captured Two Sisters and Mount Harriet in two aggressive night assaults. Other British units seized neighbouring hills and by the morning of June 14 the Argentine troops were retreating into Port Stanley. By the afternoon, the Argentines had surrendered.

The Falklands campaign was a triumph for Britain's Naval Service. The aircraft carriers, warships and submarines of the Royal Navy had achieved supremacy in the South Atlantic and provided the air defence of the landing force. The Royal Marines added to their battle honours by leading the advance on Port Stanley. Keeping the show on the road were the supply ships, oilers, and amphibious landing ships of the Royal Fleet Auxiliary. The importance of logistics in keeping

the task force fuelled and fed, 8,000 miles from its home bases cannot be overestimated. On top of this the Royal Navy had to show great innovation in rapidly requisitioning and dispatching merchant shipping to carry troops and supplies to the South Atlantic. This included converting container ships into improvised aircraft carriers so they could carry Sea Harrier and Harrier GR3 jump jets.

All of this was choreographed by senior naval officers such as Admiral Woodward and Commodore Mike Clapp. The overall commander of Operation Corporate, as the conflict was codenamed, Admiral Sir John Fieldhouse, pulled the whole British military effort together from the Royal Navy's underground command post at Northwood, outside London. Fieldhouse was subsequently appointed Chief of the Defence Staff after the conflict.

Operation Jacana

Hunting down the remnants of al-Qaeda in the high mountains of Afghanistan saw Royal Marines pushed to their limits.

ABOVE: Royal Navy submarines fired salvos of Tomahawk cruise missiles at Afghanistan in the opening days of the US invasion in October 2001. After the defeat of the Taliban government, the US, and its allies – including Britain – dispatched ground troops to hunt down and clear out the hideouts of the remnants of al-Qaeda.
(MOD/CROWN COPYRIGHT)

RIGHT: Operation Jacana saw Royal Marines heading into the mountains of eastern Afghanistan to capture and search suspected al-Qaeda hideouts.
(MOD/CROWN COPYRIGHT)

After American troops found themselves engaged in heavy fighting against al-Qaeda during Operation Anaconda in early March 2002, Britain was asked to provide a battlegroup of Royal Marines to support the US 10th Mountain and 101st Airborne Divisions in Afghanistan.

The Royal Air Force air transport fleet was called into action to move the force to Afghanistan under the code name Operation Jacana. Plans to stage flights through Karachi in Pakistan had to be rejigged after that country's government vetoed the use of the airport by British combat forces. The bulk of the Royal Marines from 3 Commando Brigade had to stage through RAFO Thumrait in Oman, as well as the existing RAF air hub at Kabul airport. To protect the inbound Hercules aircraft carrying the

Commandos and 99 Squadron's C-17s carrying cargo, all the aircraft made their flights into Afghanistan under the cover of darkness.

At the heart of Task Force Jacana was 45 Commando as the main ground combat element. It came under the umbrella of 3 Commando Brigade, commanded by Brigadier Roger Lane, with 105mm Light Guns of 29 Commando Regiment Royal Artillery and Commando Royal Engineers in support. The Commando Logistic Regiment provided essential administrative, medical, and logistic support for the British force from its main base at Bagram air base in Afghanistan, which was also the main hub of US forces in the country. Battlefield mobility was provided by the RAF's 27 Squadron with five Chinooks. The twin-rotor machines were the only helicopters that had the power and performance to carry meaningful numbers of troops and quantities of equipment up into Afghanistan's high mountain ranges. The helicopters were airlifted out to Bagram in C-17s.

The first Royal Marines' search and destroy operation was mounted in the first week of April, when a company of 40 Commando was flown by Chinook to search a cave complex in a mountainous region for al-Qaeda arms, equipment, and documents.

A week later 45 Commando launched Operation Ptarmigan, its first battalion-sized mission to search a cave complex. This was followed two weeks later by Operation Snipe, which saw the first deployment by Chinook of 105mm howitzers to support one of the search and destroy missions. During these missions, forward refuelling and arming points were established by the RAF Tactical Support Wing, including pillow tanks of fuel to reduce the need for the Chinooks to return to Bagram to refuel.

The lack of contact with hostile forces generated much frustration with the Marines and their commanders, so when Australian SAS troops came under attack near Khost on May 16, Brigadier Lane was quick to mobilise his troops to trap the suspected hostile fighters.

In a matter of hours Task Force Jacana was up and running and a constant stream of RAF and US Chinooks were lifting the Marines to their cut-off positions. US Apaches and Warthogs flew shotgun for the troop-carrying Chinooks. Despite of the rapid reaction by the Marines, the elusive enemy slipped away and Brigadier Lane's men returned to camp empty handed.

In the last week of May, the Marines deployed again but this time on a

ABOVE: RAF 27 Squadron Chinook HC2s were pushed to the limit of their performance during missions high up in the mountains of eastern Afghanistan.
(MOD/CROWN COPYRIGHT)

'hearts and minds' operation in valleys around Khost. Small groups of Marines were dropped off by Chinook to set up patrol bases to gain intelligence on al-Qaeda fighters.

On July 4, 2002, the British government announced that Task Force Jacana would return home later that month. The RAF air transport force were now called upon to fly the Royal Marines out of Afghanistan. The Marines never found their adversaries but the mission saw the first sustained use of RAF Chinooks to move combat troops around an Afghan battlefield. The environment in eastern Afghanistan was like nothing the Royal Marines had faced before and tested the endurance of the Commandos to the limit. It provided a good dry run for the return of 3 Commando Brigade to Afghanistan four years later.

LEFT: An RAF Chinook rear door gunner scans for missile threats during a mission towards the Pakistani border to drop off Royal Marines of 45 Commando during one of its search and destroy missions.
(MOD/CROWN COPYRIGHT)

Vanguard Ballistic Missile Submarines

Britain's Nuclear Deterrent

ABOVE: HMS *Victorious* heads out of Faslane on a deterrent patrol.
(MOD/CROWN COPYRIGHT)

Britain's independent nuclear deterrent is carried by the Royal Navy's four Vanguard-class ballistic missile firing nuclear-power submarines, or SSBNs to use naval jargon.

The Vanguard-class is the second generation of UK SSBNs, armed with the US-supplied Trident II, or D5, missiles. Each submarine can carry up to 16 missiles that are armed with up to eight British-designed and built thermonuclear warheads. The missiles have a range of more than 12,000 kilometres, so potentially they have the ability to strike targets in Russia or the Middle East from the North Atlantic.

Since the 1960s the UK has operated a submarine-based nuclear deterrent to make it more difficult for potential opponents to track or neutralise it. During the Cold War era, Soviet nuclear missiles could have destroyed land-based missile silos or air bases in a matter of minutes, therefore neutralising Britain's nuclear response.

By putting Britain's nuclear deterrent underwater, in effect it became invulnerable and the Soviets could not be confident of putting it out of action in a first-strike operation. The theory of mutually assured destruction, or MAD, meant that the deterrent effect of Britain's small nuclear arsenal was dramatically amplified in the face of a pre-emptive strike.

Britain's first SSBN, HMS *Resolution*, sailed on her first continuous at-sea deterrent patrols in 1969, armed with US-supplied Polaris missiles. She relieved the RAF V-bomber force of the deterrent mission. But by the late 1970s, due to the deployment of improved anti-ballistic missile defences around Moscow and enhancements to Soviet anti-

RIGHT: HMS *Vengeance*'s large missile compartment can be seen in this view of the submarine.
(MOD/CROWN COPYRIGHT)

VANGUARD CLASS

Nuclear-powered ballistic missile submarine

Builders:	Vickers Shipbuilding and Engineering, Barrow-in-Furness, Cumbria
Cost:	£15bn for four vessels
Built:	1986–1998
In service:	1993–present

Specifications

Displacement Submerged:	15,900 tons
Length:	149.9m (491ft 10in)
Beam:	12.8m (42ft)
Draught:	12m (39ft 4in)
Propulsion:	1 × Rolls-Royce PWR2 nuclear reactor
Speed:	Over 25kts (46kph; 29mph) submerged
Range/Endurance:	Limited only by food requirements and mechanical components
Complement:	135

Armament

4 × 21in (533mm) torpedo tubes for Spearfish heavyweight torpedoes

16 × ballistic missile tubes for 8–16 Lockheed Trident II D5 SLBMs (carrying up to eight warheads each)

submarine forces, a replacement was needed. In 1980 the British government selected the longer range Trident missiles to replace the old Polaris weapons and work began to design and build a British submarine to carry the weapon.

That submarine was eventually named the Vanguard-class and the keel of the first boat was laid at the then Vickers Shipbuilding and Engineering Limited's (VSEL) Barrow-in-Furness yard in Cumbria in 1986. The new submarines were significantly bigger than the old Resolution-class so VSEL's yard had to be extensively redeveloped. A new assembly building, the Devonshire Dock Hall, was built so the submarines could be assembled under cover before being lowered – rather than launched in the traditional way – into the water.

A major building programme began at the Faslane submarine base on Gare Loch in Scotland to accommodate the new Vanguard-class boats, including a new lift that would allow them to be taken out of the water for routine maintenance.

Despite the Cold War ending in 1989 with the collapse of the Berlin Wall and subsequent demise of the Soviet Union, by 1991 the British government had decided to continue with the Vanguard programme as the nation's ultimate insurance policy. No one could be sure how geo-political events would unfold. Building and operating SSBNs is a long-term endeavour that cannot be stopped or started quickly. There was some debate in the early 1990s over whether the Vanguard fleet could be trimmed down to three boats instead of the planned four, but it was decided to continue with the full programme. The cost savings were marginal against the multi-billion total cost and going down to three boats would have limited the resilience of the continuous at-sea deterrent patrols if technical problems hit one or two of the submarines.

The first of the class, HMS *Vanguard*, was launched in 1992 and commissioned a year later. A handover from the Resolution-class then began with the first one, HMS *Revenge*, retiring in 1992 and all of the old submarines being retired over the next four years. The last Vanguard-class, HMS *Vengeance*, was commissioned in 1999.

Since 1994 the Vanguard-class submarines have been continuously on patrol. The UK government never discloses any details about them or where they are operating to prevent hostile navies detecting and tracking them.

It was originally proposed that Vanguard submarines should have an operational life of around 30 years. In 2006 the British government and parliament agreed in principle to build replacement submarines to begin entering service in the early 2020s. However, in the 2010 Defence Review, on cost grounds, it was decided to continue to run the Vanguard fleet and not bring online the replacement until the end of the 2020s. »

ABOVE: HMS *Vanguard* **conducted her first deterrent patrol in 1994.** (MOD/CROWN COPYRIGHT)

LEFT: A test launch of a Trident II missile from a Royal Navy Vanguard-class submarine. (US DOD)

HMS *Vanguard*

As the first of the class, HMS *Vanguard* pioneered the entry into the service of the new type of submarine. She spent just under a decade on deterrent duty until she entered the submarine maintenance facility at Devonport dockyard in Plymouth for a major refit. This took two years and she then returned to the fleet, taking part in the firing of a Trident missile from the US Atlantic Undersea Test and Evaluation Center (AUTEC) in the Bahamas.

The submarine was involved in a remarkable incident in February 2009 while submerged in the North Atlantic when she collided with the French submarine *Le Triomphant*. How this happened has never been explained, but the damage was only minor and HMS *Vanguard* eventually returned to Faslane under her own power for a period of repairs.

In 2012, radiation was detected in the coolant plant of HMS *Vanguard*'s PWR2 nuclear reactor, caused by microscopic cracks in the fuel cladding. This prompted the submarine's recall to Devonport in 2015 for a period of deep maintenance and to be refuelled. This was only supposed to take three and half years, but the project encountered major technical problems. It was only in July 2022 that the submarine was returned to the fleet to begin shakedown trials ahead of a live missile firing later in the year.

HMS *Victorious*

The second of the Vanguard class, HMS *Victorious,* spent just over a decade on active service before entering Devonport dockyard for a major overhaul and refuelling in July 2008. This included more than 80 design additions and alterations and an upgrade to her weapons systems to improve tactical and strategic capability. Other enhancements included a new propulsor and tail shaft, a major overhaul of the generators, a survey, repair and re-preservation of the main ballast tanks, and substantial torpedo tube overhaul and upgrades.

In November 2000, the submarine was temporarily grounded on Skelmorlie Bank in the upper Firth of Clyde in Scotland, near to her Faslane home port. In 2013 she completed the 100th deterrent patrol by a Vanguard-class submarine.

HMS *VICTORIOUS*
Pennant S29
Laid down: December 3, 1987
Launched: September 29, 1993
Commissioned: January 7, 1995
Home port: HMNB Clyde
Status: Active service
Home port: HMNB Clyde
Status: Post-refit trials

HMS *VANGUARD*
Pennant S28
Ordered: May 30, 1986
Builder: Vickers Shipbuilding and Engineering Ltd, Barrow-in-Furness, Cumbria
Laid down: September 3, 1986
Launched: March 4, 1992
Commissioned: August 14, 1993
Home port: HMNB Clyde
Status: Post-refit trials

HMS *Vigilant*

The third of the Vanguard class was raided by peace protestors in 2002 who breached security at the Faslane submarine base and spray-painted graffiti slogans on her hull.

In October 2008 she entered the Devonport submarine overhaul complex for a major refit and refuelling. She returned to the fleet in 2012 and the following year test fired her main weapon system at the US underwater test range.

The submarine's captain was removed from his post in October 2017 after accusations of an inappropriate relationship with a female crew member. At the same time, HMS *Vigilant*'s executive officer was also removed from his post. Later in 2017 nine crew members were dismissed from duty on the submarine after failing drugs tests. Fleet-wide drugs tests were ordered for all Royal Navy submarine crews after the incident.

HMS *VIGILANT*
Pennant S30
Laid down: February 16, 1991
Launched: October 14, 1995
Commissioned: November 2, 1996
Home port: HMNB Clyde
Status: Active service

HMS *Vengeance*

The newest of the Vanguard class submarines was commissioned into the fleet just before the turn of the century and has seen active service since then. She suffered a technical problem with her main propeller in 2011 and had to return to Faslane on the surface.

She entered Devonport dockyard in 2012 for a 40-month long refuelling and overhaul period, including the installation of a new Trident missile launch system. The submarine left the Plymouth naval base in December 2015 to rejoin the fleet and in the first half of 2016 sailed to the east coast of the US for an extensive trials period.

This culminated in the live firing of her main weapon system from the Bahamas test range towards West Africa. The missile, minus a warhead, launched successfully from a submerged HMS *Vengeance* but the missile went off course and headed towards the coast of Florida, prompting missile controllers to destroy the weapon in flight. This was subsequently attributed to a technical issue with the test weapon rather than with HMS *Vengeance*.

HMS *VENGEANCE*
Pennant S31
Laid down: February 1, 1993
Launched: September 19, 1998
Commissioned: November 27, 1999
Home port: HMNB Clyde
Status: Active service

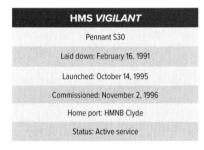

ABOVE: HMS *Vigilant* **crew rig the boat to dive.** (MOD/CROWN COPYRIGHT)

LEFT: HMS *Vengeance* **arrives at Devonport dockyard to begin an overhaul period.** (BABCOCK)

Astute Attack Submarines

The Royal Navy's Hunter Killers

Work began on the latest class of Royal Navy nuclear-powered attack submarines back in 1986 with the launching of a series of studies, known as Project SSN20, into replacement vessels for the service's Swiftsure- and Trafalgar-class boats.

This evolved into a project known initially as the Trafalgar Batch 2, but work slowed in the early 1990s after the collapse of the Berlin Wall and the end of the Cold War. UK defence spending was projected to drop by a third to secure a so-called peace dividend and highly expensive Royal Navy construction projects were put under intense scrutiny. As a result, the Ministry of Defence reduced the size of the Royal Navy submarine force, including selling off all of its Upholder-class conventionally powered submarines. The future submarine force would be entirely nuclear powered. To save money, the ministry ordered the owners of the UK's only submarine building yard, Vickers Shipbuilding and Engineering Limited (VSEL) at Barrow-in-Furness in Cumbria, to compete for the new work with a consortium led by the GEC-Marconi company.

It took until 1997 for the contract for the first three of the new attack submarines to be given to the winner of competition, GEC-Marconi. These were to be known as the Astute class. By that point GEC-Marconi had bought out VSEL and work on the submarines began at the latter's Barrow yard. The new class of submarine incorporated many of the features and systems used in the Vanguard class, including its Rolls-Royce PWR2 nuclear reactor.

The keel was not laid on the first of class, HMS *Astute*, until January 2001, as a result of delays and technical problems caused mainly by a shortage of trained design personnel. This was down to a premature run down of the submarine building programme in the early 1990s. The last Trafalgar class attack boat was commissioned in June 1991 and work on the Vanguard boats began to diminish in the middle of the decade, particularly in critical design trades.

LIVES DEPEND ON US DOING OUR JOB RIG

ASTUTE CLASS

Nuclear-powered Attack Submarine	
Builders: BAE Systems Submarines, Barrow-in-Furness, Cumbria	
Built: 2001–present	
Planned: 7	
Building: 2	
Specifications	
Displacement Submerged: 7,800 tons	
Length: 97m (318ft 3in)	
Beam: 11.3m (37ft 1in)	
Draught: 10m (32ft 10in)	
Propulsion	
1 × Rolls-Royce PWR 2 nuclear reactor	
Speed: 30kts (56kph; 35mph), submerged	
Range/Endurance: Unlimited in terms of propulsion, air, and water, but otherwise typically 90 days, based on the amount of food carried and the endurance of the crew	
Complement: 98 (with capacity for 109)	
Armament	
6 × 21in (533mm) torpedo tubes with stowage for up to 38 weapons, including a combination of Tomahawk Block IV cruise missiles and Spearfish heavyweight torpedoes	

The Astute class was designed from the start to be armed with both Spearfish heavy torpedoes to attack surface ships and other submarines and US-built Tomahawk IV land-attack missiles. It can also be fitted with a special forces delivery pod that can be installed just behind the conning tower. This allows special forces operatives to launch swimmer delivery vehicles from the submarine while it is submerged.

At the heart of the Astute class is the PWR2 nuclear reactor and the latest Core H fuel system. The latter is designed with a life of 25 years so that, in theory, the Astute boats should never have to be refuelled during their operational service. This should significantly reduce the cost of ownership of the fleet.

The submarine is fitted with the Type 2076 sonar system which, it is claimed, allows the detection and tracking of vessels at very long ranges. This brings together passive and active sonar systems, including hull and towed antenna arrays. Apparently, the system allows an Astute boat sailing in UK waters to monitor shipping traffic off the east coast of the United States.

Unfortunately, the building of the Astute class has been beset by technical delays and cost overruns and the last boat, HMS *Agincourt*, is not now expected to join the fleet until 2026. The first three boats are, in effect, a sub-class and boat number four, HMS *Audacious*, involved major changes to its internal systems, even though externally it looks little

different to its sister submarines. On current estimates, the seven Astute submarines are expected to cost £9.4 billion to build.

During the early years of service there were persistent reports that submarines had not yet achieved their top submerged speed of 30 knots. But the UK National Audit Office reported in 2015 that this key user requirement had been met.

All the Astute class submarines are based at the Faslane naval base in Scotland and a simulation facility has been built at the base to allow crews to train ahead of going to sea. This includes a simulated command centre and other facilities. »

ABOVE LEFT: Tomahawk land attack missiles are carried as standard by all Astute class submarines on operational cruises. (MOD/CROWN COPYRIGHT)

BELOW: The crew of HMS *Ambush* on deck as the submarine returns to Faslane after an operational cruise. (MOD/CROWN COPYRIGHT)

ABOVE: HMS *Astute*
returns to her home port
at Faslane naval base.
(MOD/CROWN COPYRIGHT)

HMS *Astute*

HMS *Astute* was launched by Camilla, Duchess of Cornwall in June 2007 when she pressed the button to lower the submarine into Barrow-in-Furness' Devonshire Dock. It was almost seven more years before the boat completed her extended acceptance trials process and was declared fully operational.

Her early time in service was dogged by technical problems, missteps, and a tragic shooting incident. During early trials in 2010 the submarine ran aground near the Isle of Skye, resulting in her captain being relieved of his command. A few months later, the newly repaired submarine had to return to port after the failure of her steam-generating plant. In April 2011, a drunken sailor stole a rifle and opened fire on the submarine, killing the engineering officer and wounding another crew member.

HMS *Astute* entered frontline service in 2014 and has since undertaken

multiple deployments including the 2021 Far East cruise with the carrier HMS *Queen Elizabeth*.

HMS *Ambush*

Many lessons were learnt in the building of the first of class, which enabled three years to be knocked off the process to bring HMS *Ambush* into service. She undertook weapon firing trials in 2013 and successfully fired her torpedoes and Tomahawk cruise missiles at a test range off the US East Coast.

The submarine has taken part in operational deployment around the Atlantic and Mediterranean Sea, including port visits to the United States and Brazil. In July 2016 she was damaged during a surfacing exercise near Gibraltar when she collided with a large merchant vessel.

The top of the conning tower was badly damaged and a senior officer who was on board instructing a group of trainee submarine captains was criticised in an inquiry into the incident.

HMS *AMBUSH*
Pennant number S120
Ordered: March 1997
Builder: BAE Systems Submarines, Barrow-in-Furness, Cumbria
Laid down: October 22, 2003
Launched: January 6, 2011
Commissioned: March 1, 2013
Home port: HMNB Clyde
Status: Active service

HMS *ASTUTE*
Pennant number S119
Ordered: March 1997
Builder: BAE Systems Submarines, Barrow-in-Furness, Cumbria
Laid down: January 31, 2001
Launched: June 8, 2007
Commissioned: August 27, 2010
Home port: HMNB Clyde
Status: Active service

RIGHT: HMS *Ambush*
joined the fleet in 2013.
(MOD/CROWN COPYRIGHT)

HMS *Artful*

The third of the Astute class joined the fleet as an operational vessel in 2016 and has since taken part in several operational deployments, including joining part of the Carrier Strike Group 21 mission to the Indian Ocean and Far East in the summer of 2021.

The long construction phase of the Astute class allowed the vessels to be progressively modified and HMS *Artful* was the first vessel of the class to incorporate the Common Combat System (CCS). This brings together sensor data and weapons command functions in the submarine's control room.

HMS *ARTFUL*
Pennant number S121
Ordered: March 1997
Builder: BAE Systems Submarines, Barrow-in-Furness, Cumbria
Laid down: March 11, 2005
Launched: May 17, 2014
Commissioned: March 18, 2016
Home port: HMNB Clyde
Status: Active service

HMS *Audacious*

The fourth of the Astute class is, in effect, the first of a second batch that incorporates many design and equipment changes. Her construction began in 2006 when the first long-lead items were ordered but she was not commissioned into the Royal Navy until April 2020.

Technical delays with her new equipment resulted in the submarine missing a 2018 target date to begin sea trials. She eventually sailed from Barrow-in-Furness in April 2020 and, in an unusual move, was immediately commissioned into the Royal Navy despite her constructor trials not having been completed. BAE Systems and the Royal Navy undertook a new combined constructor/acceptance trials process to speed her entry into service. »

HMS *AUDACIOUS*
Pennant number S122
Ordered: May 2007
Builder: BAE Systems Submarines, Barrow-in-Furness, Cumbria
Laid down: March 24, 2009
Launched: April 28, 2017
Commissioned: September 23, 2021
Home port: HMNB Clyde
Status: Active service

ABOVE: HMS *Artful* arrives at the British naval base on Gibraltar during a forward deployment. (GIBDAN)

BELOW: HMS *Audacious* during diving trials in the Devonshire Dock in Barrow-in-Furness. (TIM RIPLEY)

HMS *Anson*

The fifth boat of the Astute class is still at the BAE Systems shipyard at Barrow-in-Furness in the final stages of her construction. Her assembly was hit by the Covid-19 pandemic in the spring of 2020, which imposed limits on working practices inside the shipyard.

HMS *Anson* was rolled out of the Devonshire Dock assembly hall on April 19, 2021, and the following day she was lowered into the dock basin. In February 2022 she completed her first practice dive inside the dock. She was formally transferred to the Royal Navy on August 31, 2022, although she had yet to go to sea or undergo formal acceptance trials. Immediately after her commissioning, the Royal Navy said she would soon be transferred to Faslane to allow sea trails to begin. Once these have been completed it will allow the retirement of the last Trafalgar class submarine.

HMS *ANSON*
Pennant number S124
Ordered: March 2010
Builder: BAE Systems Submarines, Barrow-in-Furness, Cumbria
Laid down: October 13, 2011
Launched: April 20, 2021
Commissioned: August 31, 2022
In service: TBC
Status: Launched, fitting out

HMS *Agamemnon*

The sixth boat in the Astute class is now largely complete inside the Devonshire Hall Dock complex in Barrow-in-Furness. Her electrical power system was activated for the first time in October 2020. The next stage in her construction will be the roll and formal launch event, followed by lowering her into the Devonshire Dock. This is expected next year after HMS *Anson* sails from Barrow-in-Furness.

HMS *AGAMEMNON*
Pennant number S123
Ordered: March 2010
Builder: BAE Systems Submarines, Barrow-in-Furness, Cumbria
Laid down: July 18, 2013
In service: TBC
Status: Under construction

HMS *Agincourt*

Work on the seventh Astute class submarine is still at an early stage with construction finally being confirmed in May 2018. Long-lead items were purchased originally in 2012 but cost pressures led to consideration being given to the cancellation of the submarine in the 2010 and 2015 Defence Reviews.

Assembly work is now underway inside the Devonshire Dock Hall. This is expected to be completed early next year to allow her to be rolled out in 2024 and begin trials. The Royal Navy requires her in service no later than 2026. There is considerable pressure to complete the submarine on time to clear the Devonshire Hall Dock and allow work to move into a high gear on the first Dreadnought-class submarines. No photographs of the submarine have been released to date.

HMS *AGINCOURT*
Pennant number S125
Builder: BAE Systems Submarines, Barrow-in-Furness, Cumbria
In service: Expected between 2024 and 2026
Status: Under construction

The Last Trafalgar Class Submarine

HMS *Triumph*

The seventh and last Trafalgar-class nuclear-powered attack submarine is expected to serve on until 2024 when the fifth Astute boat, HMS *Anson,* is accepted into the fleet.

The original plan had been for HMS *Triumph* to retire by 2022 but delays to the Astute programme have meant that the Trafalgar-class submarine had to be put into an unplanned refit to allow her to remain in service for an additional two years. When she finally retires it will mark the end of the Trafalgar class, which first entered service in 1983. Her retirement will also mark the end of nuclear submarine operations from Devonport with the Astute- and Vanguard-class boats all being home based at Faslane.

HMS *Triumph* entered service in 1991 and has had a full career supporting UK interventions in Afghanistan in 2001 and Libya in 2011, firing Tomahawk land-attack missiles during both campaigns.

After her cruise into the Indian Ocean, she returned to Devonport in December 2001 flying the famous Jolly Roger pirate flag, signalling that she had taken part in a wartime mission firing an undisclosed number of Tomahawk missiles. A decade later she took part in two operational cruises off the coast of Libya and in April and June 2011 returned to Devonport again sporting Jolly Roger flags. On the first Libyan cruise she is believed to have fired six Tomahawk missiles and on the second cruise 15 missiles.

After a seven-month operational cruise in 2012, HMS *Triumph* underwent a major overhaul in Devonport dockyard in 2013.

HMS *TRIUMPH*
Pennant Number S93
Ordered: July 3, 1986
Builder: Vickers Shipbuilding and Engineering, Barrow-in-Furness, Cumbria
Laid down: February 2, 1987
Launched: February 16, 1991
Commissioned: October 2, 1991
Home port: HMNB Devonport, Plymouth
Status: Active service

ABOVE: The sun sets on HMS *Triumph*, the Royal Navy's last Trafalgar-class attack submarine. (MOD/CROWN COPYRIGHT)

BELOW: HMS *Trenchant* receives a traditional welcome after she returns to Devonport in March 2021 from her last operational cruise. (MOD/CROWN COPYRIGHT)

Queen Elizabeth-class Aircraft Carriers

A new generation of Flat Tops

The sailing of HMS *Queen Elizabeth* for her sea trials on June 26, 2017 was a major milestone in the project to close the Royal Navy's aircraft carrier gap that was created by the 2010 Strategic Defence and Security Review. As part of a bid to cut the Ministry of Defence's budget, Britain's last strike carrier, HMS *Ark Royal* and her complement of Harrier GR 9 jump jets were retired early, leaving the UK without fixed-wing naval aviation for the first time since World War One.

The money saved was to be ploughed back into making sure the delayed and over-budget HMS *Queen Elizabeth* and HMS *Prince of Wales* could actually be completed. The cost of re-establishing what is termed the UK's Carrier Enabled Power Projection (CEPP) capability is truly eye-watering, with £6.2bn needed to build the two carriers,

£5.8bn to buy 48 F-35B Lightning II joint strike fighters to fly from them and £300m to buy Crowsnest airborne early warning radars for installation in the Fleet Air Arm's Merlin HM2 helicopters.

The project was the culmination of more than 20 years of work by the Royal Navy, the British defence industry and senior government officials. Efforts to replace the old Invincible-class carriers began in the

LEFT: HMS *Queen Elizabeth* being escorted by a Type 45 air defence destroyer. (MOD/CROWN COPYRIGHT)

early 1990s and came to fruition in the 1998 Strategic Defence Review. This confirmed the requirement to build two large new aircraft carriers and for the UK to join the American Joint Strike Fighter (JSF) programme, which was in the early stages of building a replacement for the AV-8B Harrier and other combat aircraft. The JSF eventually became the F-35B Lightning.

The aircraft carrier programme formally kicked off in 1999 when the Ministry of Defence contracted two teams, British Aerospace (now BAE Systems) and Thomson-CSF (now Thales) to prepare rival designs. In January 2003, the ministry picked the Thales design as the best but said it wanted BAE Systems to build the ships in their yards. This set in motion the formation of what

became known as the Aircraft Carrier Alliance, comprising BAE Systems, Thales and Babcock International. The maritime repair and services company was needed because it owned the Rosyth dockyard, a former Royal Navy base, which was the only naval shipyard in Britain with a big enough dry dock for the new 65,000 ton carriers to be assembled. »

BELOW: Babcock's Rosyth shipyard in Scotland won the contract to provide long-term maintenance for the Queen Elizabeth-class carriers because it is one of the few yards in the UK with a big enough dry dock to take the giant ships out of the water. (BABCOCK)

ABOVE: The Royal Navy intends to alternate having HMS *Queen Elizabeth* and HMS *Prince of Wales* at high readiness for operations. (MOD/CROWN COPYRIGHT)

A major part of the process in finalising the design was working out how to physically construct such a big ship. It was eventually decided to go for a block assembly process that saw several shipyards around Britain being contracted to build sections of the carrier. These blocks would be pre-assembled with all the piping, decking, cabling, and major components and then shipped on giant barges to Rosyth where they would be welded together to create fully formed aircraft carriers.

This was a revolutionary way of building large warships and it meant a considerable proportion of the work on the carriers was conducted away from Rosyth. The two new carriers were the largest warships to be built since the 53,000 ton Audacious-class carriers in the 1940s and 1950s, so the UK shipbuilding industry largely had to start from scratch to work out how to build the ships.

After the first steel was cut in 2009, work accelerated, and by the time HMS *Queen Elizabeth* was launched in 2014 it was too late to go back. In 2014 it was finally confirmed that HMS *Prince of Wales* would be brought into service on a full-time basis to allow the Royal Navy to maintain a continuous at-sea carrier presence. In the following year's Defence Review, the purchase of the full complement of 48 F-35Bs was confirmed which allowed both carriers to simultaneously embark at least one squadron of the jets.

Not surprisingly, HMS *Queen Elizabeth*'s first commanding officer, Commodore Jerry Kyd, said in 2017 that the cost and hard work involved in getting her to sea would be worth the effort. "The premier nations of the world are investing billions of dollars in aircraft carriers," he said on the bridge of his ship, just before she was to sail for the first time. "The ship will provide the British government with an incredibly flexible tool. We are globally outward nations. HMS *Queen Elizabeth* and her sister ship, HMS *Prince of Wales*, are to give Britain a global presence. Anywhere she goes in world it will give Britain a serious punch."

The 65,000-ton HMS *Queen Elizabeth* was manoeuvred out of the dockyard's basin on June 26, 2017, and later that evening passed under the three major bridges across the Firth of Forth to start her four-month contractors' trials programme to allow her to be handed over to the Royal Navy.

Eleven tugs were used to move the 280m long ship out of the Aircraft Carrier Alliance's basin at Rosyth and position her in the Firth before she started to pass beneath the bridges.

RIGHT: HMS *Queen Elizabeth* and HMS *Prince of Wales* were briefly both at sea together in May 2021. (MOD/CROWN COPYRIGHT)

The need to bring HMS *Queen Elizabeth* into dry dock for inspection, overhaul, and capability insertion meant that the second carrier had to be online to cover any gaps. France had only been able to afford to build one nuclear-powered aircraft carrier in the 1980s and 1990s and this meant there were lengthy periods when she was not available for operations.

"Two carriers mean continuous availability so politicians can decide how to use them," said HMS *Prince of Wales'* senior naval officer, Captain Ian Groom in 2017. "Politicians need to have carrier strike available at the time of their choosing – they need HMS *Prince of Wales* to give them that."

The completion of HMS *Prince of Wales* followed along in the wake of HMS *Queen Elizabeth*, and she was formally accepted in Royal Navy service in December 2019. This meant the process of regenerating the Royal Navy's carrier strike capability was initially set for December 2020 and full operating capability due by 2023.

A key part of bringing the two carriers into service was the integration of the aircraft and naval air squadrons on board the ships, as

LEFT: The Queen Elizabeth-class aircraft carriers are designed with command-and-control facilities to allow them to lead multi-national naval task forces. (MOD/CROWN COPYRIGHT)

QUEEN ELIZABETH-CLASS

Displacement: 65,000 tons
Length: 280m (919ft)
Beam: 73m (240ft)
Draught: 11m (36ft)
Speed: 25kts (46kph; 29mph)
Capacity: 1,600, of which 679 are usually the ship's crew
Armament: three Phalanx CIWS, four 30mm DS30M Mk2 guns and six mini-guns
Aircraft carried: 40 aircraft and helicopters (65+ aircraft surge capacity)

well as training to operate as a fully-fledged carrier battle group. This was particularly important for the F-35B, which had never operated from any Royal Navy ship before and involved revolutionary lift-fan technology. The ship's decks had been protected by specially designed heat-resistant coatings, but this had never been tested on a ship at sea.

HMS *Queen Elizabeth* first went to the east coast of the United States of America for F-35B integration trials run by the US Navy's Air Systems Command and the aircraft's manufacturer, Lockheed Martin. This involved specially instrumented aircraft making the first deck landings and take-offs from the ship. The next phase involved work-up training with in-service aircraft from the RAF's 617 Squadron in US and home waters.

Training the ship's crews to operate her systems and work on her flight deck was just as important as training the aircrew. A mock aircraft carrier deck was laid out at RNAS Culdrose to help train up deck crews and aircraft handlers.

Major investments were also made at HM Naval Base Portsmouth to make it the home port of the carriers. This included additional dredging of the harbour channel to allow the carriers to enter the base, as well as dock-side infrastructure. A new jetty was built at Glen Mallan on Loch Long to allow ammunition from the Glen Douglas ordnance depot, including aircraft bombs and missiles, to be loaded onto the new carriers.

Building the Queen Elizabeth-class aircraft carriers has been a national project and they will remain in service for several generations.

BELOW: HMS *Queen Elizabeth* approaches the Glenn Mallan ordnance depot in Scotland to take on ammunition ahead of the Carrier Strike Group 21 deployment. (MOD/CROWN COPYRIGHT)

HMS
Queen Elizabeth

The Royal Navy's Flagship

ABOVE: HMS *Queen Elizabeth*'s **distinctive stern as she left Portsmouth for the Carrier Strike Group 21 deployment.**
(MOD/CROWN COPYRIGHT)

RIGHT: HMS *Queen Elizabeth*'s **badge harks back to the Tudor monarch she is named after.**
(TIM RIPLEY)

HMS *Queen Elizabeth* has been the Royal Navy's flagship since January 27, 2021, when she took over the highly symbolic role from the amphibious dock ship HMS *Albion*. This was the culmination of more than 20 years of effort to field the Royal Navy's new class of aircraft carriers.

The first of the new Queen Elizabeth-class aircraft carriers was named after the World War One-era super-dreadnought battleship, HMS *Queen Elizabeth*, which in turn was named after the Tudor monarch, Queen Elizabeth, who famously oversaw the defeat of the Spanish Armada in 1588. The modern HMS *Queen Elizabeth* carries the battle honours and crest – a Tudor rose – of the original battleship.

She is the largest-ever Royal Navy warship and the most expensive surface ship yet built in the United Kingdom. After a decade of development and design work, the formal go-ahead for the two 65,000 ton Queen Elizabeth-class aircraft carriers was announced in July 2007. The two ships were contracted to cost £3.9 billion. Work began on the construction of HMS *Queen Elizabeth* in July 2009 with the first steel being cut at BAE Systems' Govan shipyard in Glasgow.

The first phase of the project included the fabrication of ship blocks at six shipyards around the UK, each of which incorporated key structural elements as well as piping and electrical wiring. The blocks were then floated on large barges to Babcock International's Rosyth dockyard in

Fife, where the final assembly of the ship was conducted by BAE Systems and Babcock under the umbrella of the Aircraft Carrier Alliance.

The first two blocks were welded together at Rosyth in June 2011 and over the next two years the ship took shape. She was 80% complete by September 2013 and was formally named HMS *Queen Elizabeth* on July 4, 2014. Thirteen days later she was floated out of the Rosyth dry dock in the shipyard's basin to allow the final fitting out to begin.

This activity had largely been completed by mid-2017 and on June 26, 2017, she was manoeuvred out of the basin into the Firth of Forth to begin her contractors' sea trials. After a brief visit to Invergordon anchorage the following month to inspect possible damage to her propeller shafts, she set sail for her new home at HM Naval Base Portsmouth and arrived on August 16. The ship was formally accepted by the Royal Navy on December 7 during a ceremony while she was docked at Portsmouth. The final costs of the two Queen Elizabeth-class carriers have now been confirmed by the Ministry of Defence to be £6.1bn.

After three years of trials and work-up training in UK waters and off the east coast of the United States of America, HMS *Queen Elizabeth* sailed on her maiden operational deployment, dubbed Carrier Strike Group 21. This ambitious deployment took the carrier into the Mediterranean, Indian Ocean, and Eastern Pacific. For the deployment, a multi-national task group was formed that included a Dutch frigate, a US destroyer, and a US Marine Corps F-35B squadron. The Royal Navy supported the carrier with two Type 45 air defence destroyers, two Type 23 frigates, two Royal Fleet Auxiliary support ships and an Astute-class nuclear-powered attack submarine.

The deployment also saw the operational debut of the Crowsnest early warning variant of the Merlin HM2 maritime helicopter and the Martlet anti-ship missiles fitted to the Wildcat HMA2 light helicopter.

There had been speculation that the carrier group would be embroiled in a confrontation with the Chinese navy off Taiwan when it transited northwards en route to Japan, but the passage was completed without incident.

When returning home via the Mediterranean, the carrier suffered her first-ever aircraft loss when an RAF F-35B suffered an engine failure as it approached the ski jump during take-off. The pilot was able to successfully eject from the stricken jet but his parachute was briefly entangled on the bow of the ship.

After returning to Portsmouth in December 2020, the ship entered a period of regeneration for several months. She was scheduled to return to frontline operational service in late 2022 and take her air group on exercise to the Mediterranean and Baltic Seas to train with NATO forces. This plan was re-jigged in September 2022 when her sister ship, HMS *Prince of Wales*, suffered a technical problem en route to the United States and HMS *Queen Elizabeth* had to step in to take her place.

ABOVE: HMS *Queen Elizabeth* met her sister ship HMS *Prince of Wales* off the Scottish coast in May 2021 before the Royal Navy flagship headed to the Far East. (MOD/CROWN COPYRIGHT)

LEFT: F-35B Lightning II jump jets are a core part of the HMS *Queen Elizabeth* air group. (MOD/CROWN COPYRIGHT)

HMS
Prince of Wales

The Royal Navy's Second Aircraft Carrier

BELOW LEFT: The sail of HMS *Prince of Wales* against the backdrop of the Aurora Borealis during a visit to the Arctic Circle for Exercise Cold response in March 2022. (MOD/CROWN COPYRIGHT)

BELOW RIGHT: The bridge of HMS *Prince of Wales*, sporting her name plate and R09 pennant number. (TIM RIPLEY)

The sister ship of HMS *Queen Elizabeth* is rapidly gaining a reputation for being the most unreliable warship in the fleet, despite being its newest vessel. Over the past two years she has been hit by two major technical problems that have prevented her meeting important operational commitments.

She is named after the World War Two battleship, HMS *Prince of Wales* that was famously sunk by Japanese torpedo bombers in December 1941 off the coast of Malaya. She is the eighth Royal Navy warship to bear the name, which is the title traditionally given to the heir apparent to the British throne.

Since the sinking of the previous HMS *Prince of Wales* no vessels have carried the name, such was the shock caused by the sinking of the battleship in the dark days before the fall of Britain's imperial bastion of Singapore.

The Queen Elizabeth-class carriers were built deliberately as a pair so that one of the two ships would always be ready for operations. HMS *Prince of Wales* was built to the same basic design as HMS *Queen Elizabeth* and was assembled in the same shipyard in Fife, using the same modular construction process.

Work on HMS *Prince of Wales* began in May 2011 with the first steel being cut at BAE Systems' Govan shipyard in Glasgow. The first blocks arrived at Babcock's Rosyth yard in September 2014 and assembly accelerated until she was floated out of the dry dock into the basin towards the end of 2017 to allow final fitting out.

She was ready to sail on September 29, 2019 and passed out of the basin into the Firth of Forth to begin her contractors' sea trials. Once the carrier had arrived at HM Naval Base Portsmouth she was formally commissioned into the Royal Navy. In February 2020 the ship made a week-long visit to the port of Liverpool and hosted thousands of visitors on board in a major exercise in public engagement.

However, HMS *Prince of Wales* suffered her first major technical problem in May 2020 after returning to her home port at Portsmouth when she suffered the first of two floods in her engine room as a result of leaks linked to her propulsion system.

In October 2020, the ship was hit by a more significant leak that caused a major flooding in her engine room. This led to damage to electrical cabling and the electrical generator that transferred power to her propellers. By the end of 2020, the damage had been revealed as being serious and an eight-month programme of repairs began. This led to the carrier's deployment to the east coast of the US for Lockheed Martin F-35B Lightning II jump jet trials to be cancelled.

The repairs had been completed by April 2021 when HMS *Prince of Wales* sailed for a new round of sea trials. These apparently concluded that the problems had been solved and she was declared operational on October 31, 2021.

During January 2022 she set sail for a series of major UK and NATO naval exercises off Scotland and Norway. These coincided with the ship taking up the role of the flagship of the naval component of the NATO Response Force.

The ship then began preparing for a four-month deployment to the east coast of the US. This involved an ambitious programme of exercises with US and Canadian militaries, including the launching of jet-powered Banshee unmanned aerial vehicles from the carrier's deck. This was to simulate the carrier's battle group coming under attack from high performance aircraft and missiles. The carrier was also scheduled to conduct Shipborne Vertical Rolling Landing (SRVL) trials for her F-35Bs. This technique allows a carrier's jets to land on board with a full bomb load, preventing them having to dump very expensive unused missiles and guided bombs in the sea before landing. The final element of the deployment was supposed to be the hosting of the Atlantic Future Forum in New York, where the city's political and diplomatic elite would visit the ship. The whole programme was thrown into doubt, though, on August 27, 2022 when HMS *Prince of Wales* suffered a major failure of her starboard propeller shaft. For several days she was at anchor off the Isle of Wight while divers and engineers inspected her engines and propellers before a decision was made on September 2 for her to return to port for repairs.

ABOVE: The first hull blocks of HMS *Prince of Wales* were brought together at Rosyth shipyard in December 2014. (AIRCRAFT CARRIER ALLIANCE)

BELOW: HMS *Prince of Wales* sailing north to Exercise Cold Response off Norway in March, 2022 in order to train with NATO forces. (MOD/CROWN COPYRIGHT)

Albion-class Dock Ships

Putting the Royal Marines Ashore

Delivering amphibious forces to operational areas is a complex and difficult endeavour that requires specialist shipping. The Royal Navy and Royal Marines have learnt this lesson the hard way through bitter experience in many campaigns stretching back to the ill-fated Gallipoli landings in World War One.

The critical manoeuvre is the delivery of troops and their equipment to the beach from large ocean-going ships. This requires plenty of landing craft but also dedicated vessels that can safely load troops into the landing craft and then launch them on their way to the shore.

During World War Two the US Navy developed the first landing ships with their own internal, or well, dock that could carry landing craft across the Pacific before beach assault operations. This proved far more effective than trying to drop landing craft down the side of cargo ships on cranes.

The Royal Navy got its first purpose-built landing ship docks (LSDs) in the early 1960s when HMS *Fearless* and HMS *Intrepid* entered service. They successfully launched their landing craft into action in 1982 in San Carlos Water during the Falklands Conflict.

In the 1990s a project to replace the two ships was launched and this culminated in 1996 with an order being placed with the then Vickers Shipbuilding and Engineering Limited, now BAE Systems, in Barrow-in-Furness, Cumbria, to build two new Albion class LSDs.

ALBION CLASS

Landing Platform Dock

Builders: BAE Systems Marine	
Cost: £225m per unit	
Built: 2	

Specifications

Displacement: 19,560 tons	
Length: 176m (577ft)	
Beam: 28.9m (95ft)	
Draught: 7.1m (23ft)	
Propulsion: GE Power Conversion Full Electric Propulsion System	
Speed: 18kts (33kph; 21mph)	
Range: 8,000 miles (7,000nm; 13,000km)	
Crew Complement: 325	
Boats & landing craft carried includes 4 × LCU MK10, 4 × LCVP MK5	
Capacity: 67 vehicles, 405 Royal Marines (710 surge)	

Armament

2 × 20mm Phalanx CIWS, 2 × 20 mm cannon,
4 × General Purpose Machine Guns

Aviation facilities:

Two landing spots for helicopters up to the
size of a Chinook.

The ships were designed to function as the afloat command platform for amphibious task force and landing force command staff when embarked, as well as to embark, transport, deploy and recover amphibious troops along with their equipment and vehicles.

As well as a large helicopter deck and purpose-designed command and control facilities, the ships have a large well dock that can hold four Landing Craft Utility (LCU) Mark 10s and four smaller Landing Craft Vehicle Personnel (LCVP) Mark 5s. There is an internal articulated ramp that leads up to the ship's vehicle deck and allows the landing craft to be loaded within the sheltered well dock before they exit from the rear gate. Each ship also carries a 52-ton tracked beach recovery vehicle for assisting with landing craft recovery, as well as two tractors – one that can lay a trackway across a landing beach and the second fitted with an excavating bucket and forks.

The design of the ships is inherently flexible, allowing assault troops to be loaded on landing craft or carried ashore by helicopter. In surge mode more than 400 troops can be carried aboard each ship.

However, the ships do not have hanger decks to allow helicopters to be maintained in heavy weather and rough seas. They were ordered soon after the Royal Navy's new helicopter carrier, HMS *Ocean*, entered service and that ship was intended to be the home of an amphibious force's rotary wing element.

The new dock ships entered service just after the 2003 Iraq war and then took part in several major exercises, proving to be robust and effective. The 2010 defence cuts considerably reduced the UK's high readiness amphibious forces and to save money it was decided to keep only one of the

LSD in frontline service. The ships alternate between what is termed "extended readiness periods" in Devonport dockyard. This is usually around two years at a time, although the Royal Navy said in time of crisis the tied-up ship can be brought back into service rapidly. In practice, as the main problem is a lack of sailors to crew the ships, this situation is considered highly unlikely and since 2010 the Royal Navy has never operated more than one of the ships at a time.

ABOVE: The large dock on the Albion class landing ships provides a home for a variety of landing craft and small boats operated by the Royal Marines. (MOD/CROWN COPYRIGHT)

BELOW: As well as its dock, the Albion class also has a large helicopter landing deck to allow vertical assault operations to be launched from the ships. (MOD/CROWN COPYRIGHT)

HMS *Albion*

Amphibious Stalwart

ABOVE: An RAF Chinook heavy lift helicopter landing on HMS *Albion* during an amphibious warfare exercise in 2008.
(MOD/CROWN COPYRIGHT)

The latest HMS *Albion* took on the traditions of the Centaur-class aircraft carrier which had been converted into a commando carrier in 1962 and after extensive service retired a decade later as Britain wound up its Empire 'East of Suez'.

The new HMS *Albion* entered service just after the 2003 Iraq war and was soon committed to a series of major exercises. During the 2006 Vela Deployment to West Africa it functioned as the Amphibious Task Group flagship, controlling 3,000 British personnel and 11 ships of the Royal Navy and Royal Fleet Auxiliary. In April 2010, during the air travel disruption caused by the eruption of the Eyjafjallajökull volcano in Iceland, HMS *Albion* was sent to Santander in northern Spain to bring home stranded UK nationals and British military personnel.

In March 2011 she operated as part of the Royal Navy Response Force Task Group in the Gulf of Sidra, off Libya, to aid the ongoing NATO-led mission to protect the country's civilian population from Colonel Gaddafi's troops.

RIGHT: HMS *Albion* decked out to celebrate the late Queen's 96th birthday in April 2022.
(MOD/CROWN COPYRIGHT)

As a result of the 2010 defence cuts, the Royal Navy was only allowed to operate one of the Albion class LSDs at a time. It was HMS *Albion*'s turn to enter extended readiness in late 2011. In December 2014, HMS *Albion* was moved into dry dock at Plymouth to allow her hull to be inspected and cleaned prior to major work being undertaken during the reactivation of the ship. This considerable refit, plus the associated work-up period, took 30 months and so it was not until April 2017 that HMS *Albion* assumed the role of Fleet Flagship.

In September 2020, *Albion* embarked on a Littoral Response Group (Experimentation) [LRG(X)] deployment to conduct a training exercise in the Mediterranean with Royal Marine Commando forces and Royal Naval personnel. In January 2021, HMS *Albion* transferred Fleet Flagship duty to HMS *Queen Elizabeth*.

HMS *ALBION*
Pennant Number: L14
Ordered: July 18, 1996
Builder: BAE Systems Marine, Barrow-in-Furness, Cumbria
Laid down: May 23, 1998
Launched: March 9, 2001
Commissioned: June 19, 2003
Home port: HMNB Devonport, Plymouth
Status: Active service

HMS *Bulwark*

At the heart of the Amphibious Fleet

HMS *Bulwark* sailed in January 2006 for a six-month maiden cruise east of Suez and conducted counterterrorist and counter-piracy tasks in waters off the Horn of Africa. She then headed for the northern Persian Gulf to become the flagship of Task Force 158, providing security for Iraqi oil platforms. Later in 2006 she was diverted to the Mediterranean to help with the evacuation of British citizens from the conflict in Lebanon.

After a major refit, HMS *Bulwark* was returned to duty in late 2011 and took over as the fleet flagship from HMS *Albion*, which had entered extended readiness. Over the next four years HMS *Bulwark* was highly active in support of British and NATO exercises.

Between April and July 2015, HMS *Bulwark* played a major part in European Union search and rescue operation off the Italian coast, under the codename Operation Weald, to assist migrants in distress crossing from Libya. During this mission, she recovered over 2,900 migrants from the sea.

In late 2017, HMS *Bulwark* returned to extended readiness and handed the baton as fleet flagship back to HMS *Albion*. During 2020 the ship was dry-docked for phase two of her optimised support period. She remained in dry dock prior to undertaking a phase 3 recertification package ahead of her planned return to the fleet in 2023.

The future of UK amphibious forces has been at the centre of debates in the Ministry of Defence for several years and there have been repeated reports that one or both of the LPDs could be sacrificed to save money. The Royal Navy and Royal Marines are now focused on the Littoral Strike Ship concept to forward-deploy amphibious forces in future crisis zones, using the two Albion class LSDs and the Bay-class landing ships, as well as RFA *Argus*.

HMS *BULWARK*		
Pennant Number: L15		
Ordered: July 18, 1996		
Builder: BAE Systems Marine, Barrow-in-Furness, Cumbria		
Laid down: January 27, 2000		
Launched: November 15, 2001		
Commissioned: April 28, 2005		
Home port: HMNB Devonport, Plymouth		
Status: At extended readiness		

ABOVE: In 2015 HMS *Bulwark* was dispatched to the central Mediterranean to help rescue migrants trying to escape from war-torn Libya. (MOD/CROWN COPYRIGHT)

LEFT: HMS *Bulwark* commanded a naval task force during Exercise Joint Warrior 2013 off the coast of Scotland, controlling surface vessels, submarines, air assets and amphibious forces. (MOD/CROWN COPYRIGHT)

Type 45 Destroyers

Defender of the Fleet

The Type 45 is the Royal Navy's primary destroyer, intended to provide wide-area air defence for naval task groups using its Principal Anti-Air Missile System (PAAMS) which fires Sea Viper missiles.

During the 1990s the UK had been working with France and Italy on a new class of warship to be equipped with the PAAMS weapon that was also being jointly developed by the three nations. The UK subsequently decided to go its own way on the ship element of the project. In 1999 Marconi Electronic Systems was selected to be the prime contractor on the new class of ships at a projected cost of

£5 billion, although that figure later rose to more than £6.4 billion. Later the same year, Marconi merged with British Aerospace to create a new company, BAE Systems, and its maritime division subsequently took over responsibility for building the new ships at its yards in Govan and Scotstoun on the Clyde. Initially, BAE Systems worked in co-operation with the VT Group – formerly Vosper Thornycroft – which owned a shipyard in Portsmouth. In 2009, BAE Systems took over VT Group and gained full control of the Type 45 programme.

The Type 45, or Daring Class, represented a step change in warship design and construction and it also transformed the air defence capability of the Royal Navy. It was the first Royal Navy warship to incorporate electric drive rather than traditional propeller shafts linked to the main engine. This new technology was supposed to be more reliable and reduce the need for mechanical components, easing maintenance and reducing the size of engine compartments. Ship designers around the world had been looking at integrated electric propulsion systems in the 1990s, and the Royal Navy was in the first wave of navies to adopt the technology.

Marconi and then BAE Systems, as well as VT, also proposed a revolutionary method of constructing the vessels, splitting work between three main yards – Govan, Scotstoun and Portsmouth. Each of the yards

TYPE 45 GUIDED MISSILE DESTROYER

Builders: BAE Systems Maritime – Naval Ships

Cost: £6.46bn total

Built: 2003–2010

Completed: 6

Specifications

Displacement: 8,500 tonnes

Length: 152.4m (500ft)

Beam: 21.2m (69ft 7in)

Draught: 7.4m (24ft 3in)

Propulsion:

2 × Rolls-Royce WR-21 gas turbines, 21.5 MW (28,800shp)

2 × Wärtsilä 12V200 diesel generators, 2 MW (2,700shp)

Speed: In excess of 32kts (59kph; 37mph)

Range: In excess of 7,000nm (13,000km)

Complement: 191 (accommodation for up to 285)

Sensors

SAMPSON multi-function air-tracking radar (Type 1045)

S1850M 3-D air-surveillance radar (Type 1046)

Armament

Anti-air missiles: PAAMS air-defence system comprising 48 × Sylver Vertical Launching System A50 for combination of Aster 15 missiles (range 1.7–30km) and Aster 30 missiles (range 3–120km)

Anti-ship missiles: Up to 4 × 8 Harpoon missiles

Guns: 1 × 4.5in Mark 8 naval gun, 2 × 30mm DS30B guns, 2 × 20mm Phalanx CIWS, 2 × Miniguns, 6 × 7.62mm General Purpose Machine Guns

Aviation Facilities

Chinook-capable flight deck and enclosed hangar

Aircraft carried: 1 × Wildcat HMA2 or 1 × Merlin HM2

was charged with pre-building ship hull blocks, which were then moved to Govan on giant barges where they were joined together in a ship assembly hall. Final outfitting with the main weapons and sensors took place at Scotstoun. This was the first time the construction method had been used for Royal Navy warships, and it was subsequently used in the construction of the two Queen Elizabeth-class aircraft carriers.

The PAAMS system transformed the air defence capabilities of the Royal Navy by allowing targets to be engaged at more significant ranges than the old Sea Dart missiles on the Type 42 destroyers, which were the ships the Type 45s were intended to replace. This new missile, and its associated Samson radar, could detect and engage more targets at longer range.

When the Type 45s were first ordered in 1999, the intention was to build 12 ships to replace the Type 42s, but as costs escalated on the project during the early phases of the new ships' construction, pressure grew to cap spending. So, in 2008, the decision was made to cease construction after only six had been built.

The first of this class, HMS *Daring*, was commissioned into Royal Navy service in 2009 and the last vessel entered service four years later. As the ships were deployed on operations further from home, it became apparent that the integrated electric propulsion systems were suffering from major reliability problems. This culminated in a series of incidents in which Type 45s completely lost power when the electric generators tripped out. In a bid to resolve the problem, the Ministry of Defence approved a £160 million project, dubbed the Power Improvement Project (PIP), to install new electric generators. This involved major engineering modifications to remove the old generators and install the new systems. To date only one of the Type 45s, HMS *Dauntless*, has successfully had the new equipment fitted and, under current plans, the last of the ships will not be modified until 2028.

HMS *Daring*

As the first in the class, HMS *Daring* underwent an intense period of trials to prove that her new and innovative systems worked as advertised. She was officially declared fit for operations in July 2010 and fired her first-ever Sea Viper missile in May 2011. The ship sailed for her maiden operational cruise in January 2012.

HMS *Daring* was laid up from 2017 to 2020 because of a shortage of naval personnel to crew her. In 2021 she was towed to Cammell Laird's yard in Birkenhead to allow new diesel generators to be installed under the Power Improvement Project which would rectify issues with the Type 45s' electric drive system. As early as 2010, HMS *Daring* had suffered a total power loss in the Atlantic.

HMS *DARING*		
Pennant Number D32		
Ordered: December 20, 2000		
Builder: BAE Systems Naval Ships, Govan and Scotstoun, Glasgow		
Laid down: March 28, 2003		
Launched: February 1, 2006		
Commissioned: July 23, 2009		
Home port: HMNB Portsmouth		
Status: Undergoing Type 45 Power Improvement Project (PIP) conversion at Cammell Laird, Birkenhead		

HMS *Dauntless*

Although the second in class, HMS *Dauntless* was the first Type 45 destroyer to live-fire the Sea Viper missile system in June 2010 during her acceptance trials.

In 2015 she sailed on a cruise to the Middle East and was assigned to work with the USS *Carl Vinson* task group, providing air defence protection for the US aircraft carrier.

A shortage of naval personnel resulted in her being withdrawn from frontline service in 2016 and she was

HMS *DAUNTLESS*		
Pennant Number D33		
Ordered: December 20, 2000		
Builder: BAE Systems Surface Fleet Solutions, Govan and Scotstoun, Glasgow		
Laid down: August 28, 2004		
Launched: January 23. 2007		
Commissioned: June 3, 2010		
Home port: HMNB Portsmouth		
Status: Active service		

used as a training ship in Portsmouth dockyard for four years. In 2020 she become the prototype vessel for the Power Improvement Project which aimed to solve the problems with the Type 45s' electric drive system. This was completed in June 2022.

HMS *Diamond*

In 2012 the ship sailed for her first operational deployment, which took her to the Middle East. The technical problems that plagued the Type 45-class hit HMS *Diamond* in November 2017 when she was en route to the Indian Ocean. The crew could not resolve the problems with her propulsion systems and she had to return to Portsmouth.

In 2021, as the ship was passing through the Mediterranean to the Far East as part of the Carrier Strike Group 21 deployment, one of her gas turbines failed and she had to put into Taranto in Italy for repairs. She later caught up with the task group but was again hit by technical problems and had to put into Singapore to resolve them.

HMS *DIAMOND*		
Pennant Number D34		
Ordered: December 20, 2000		
Builder: BAE Systems Surface Fleet Solutions, Govan and Scotstoun, Glasgow		
Laid down: February 25, 2005		
Launched: November 27, 2007		
Commissioned: May 6, 2011		
Home port: HMNB Portsmouth		
Status: Active service		

HMS *Dragon*

HMS *Dragon* has proved to be one of the most reliable – and hence most active – Type 45 destroyers.

After joining the fleet in April 2012, she deployed on operational duty on an annual basis. In 2013 she was in the Middle East during the Syria crisis and the following year headed to the South Atlantic.

She participated in the rescue of a stricken ocean-racing yacht in February 2017. During a maritime security mission in the Middle East in 2018, her Royal Marines detachment seized a large quantity of illicit drugs.

The following year the ship was at the centre of operations in the Strait of Hormuz during rising tension with Iran.

HMS DRAGON	
Pennant Number D35	
Ordered: December 20, 2000	
Builder: BVT Surface Fleet, Portsmouth	
Laid down: December 19, 2005	
Launched: November 17, 2008	
Commissioned: April 20, 2012	
Home port: HMNB Portsmouth	
Status: Active service	

HMS *Defender*

The destroyer was declared ready for active service in November 2013 and within weeks engaged in escorting the Russian aircraft carrier, RFS *Admiral Kuznetsov,* through UK waters.

In 2014, she deployed to the Middle East to work as an air defence escort for a US aircraft carrier task group and she repeated the role in 2015 in support of the French carrier, FS *Charles de Gaulle* off the coast of Syria.

During June 2021, HMS *Defender* engaged in a major confrontation with Russian warships and aircraft in the Black Sea after the British government ordered her to sail through waters near Crimea claimed by Moscow. A Russian warship fired warning shots in proximity to the ship and she was buzzed at low level by Russian fighter jets.

HMS DEFENDER	
Pennant Number D36	
Ordered: December 20, 2000	
Builder: BAE Systems Surface Ships, Govan and Scotstoun, Glasgow	
Laid down: July 31, 2006	
Launched: October 21, 2009	
Commissioned: March 21, 2013	
Home port: HMNB Portsmouth	
Status: Active service	

HMS *Duncan*

HMS *Duncan* deployed on her first operational cruise in March 2015 when she headed to the Middle East to escort a US Navy aircraft carrier battle group.

The following year she escorted the Russian aircraft carrier, RFS *Admiral Kuznetsov,* through the English Channel as the ship headed to Syria. Later in 2016 the ship suffered a total propulsion failure and had to be towed back to Portsmouth for repairs.

As tension mounted with Iran in the summer of 2019, HMS *Duncan* was diverted from a deployment in the Black Sea to the Arabian Gulf to support HMS *Montrose* which had been involved in several incidents with Iranian gunboats.

HMS DUNCAN	
Pennant Number D37	
Ordered: December 20, 2000	
Builder: BAE Systems Surface Ships, Govan and Scotstoun, Glasgow	
Laid down: January 26, 2007	
Launched: October 11, 2010	
Commissioned: September 26, 2013	
Home port: HMNB Portsmouth	
Status: Active service	

ABOVE: HMS *Dragon* featured in the 2021 James Bond movie *No Time to Die.* (MOD/CROWN COPYRIGHT)

BELOW LEFT: HMS *Defender* duelled with Russian jets in the Black Sea in 2021. (MOD/CROWN COPYRIGHT)

BELOW RIGHT: HMS *Duncan* is the newest Type 45 destroyer. (MOD/CROWN COPYRIGHT)

Type 23 Frigates

General Purpose Frigate

Not surprisingly, the Type 23 general purpose frigates are often described as the 'workhorses of the Royal Navy'. The 12 surviving Royal Navy Type 23s are the service's most reliable and effective surface vessels. Due to issues impacting on the Type 45 destroyers' new electric drive systems, the Type 23s are often called upon whenever the Royal Navy has to deploy warships in response to unforeseen events or crises.

The Type 23, or Duke Class, originated at the height of the Cold War in the early 1980s and were designed by the Royal Corps of Naval Constructors (RCNC). They were responsible at that time for producing warship designs and shipyards and would then compete to win orders to build them. This was an era when the British shipbuilding industry was flush with warship orders from the Royal Navy and there was little incentive for shipyards to secure export orders or modify their designs to meet the needs of foreign navies. Eventually, Type 23 construction was divided between the then Yarrow Yard on the Clyde (now BAE Systems') and Swan Hunter in

Tyneside, which has since gone out of business.

From the start, the Royal Navy wanted the future Type 23 to lead its anti-submarine warfare operations in the North Atlantic to counter the growing Soviet submarine threat. It was the first Royal Navy warship designed to be equipped with towed sonar arrays from the start. In the early 1980s these were seen as key to outsmarting the latest generation of ultra-quiet Soviet submarines. Trailing the sonar array thousands of metres behind the frigate moved it away from the noise generated by the

ship's engines and machinery. This allowed sonar operators to pick up the sound of enemy submarines at very long distances.

The Type 23's own noise signature was in turn reduced by its combined diesel-electric and gas (CODLAG) propulsion system that provided incredibly quiet running for anti-submarine operations.

It was intended that the ship would replace three existing classes of frigates – the Leanders, Type 21s and Type 22s – in a bid to dramatically reduce training, logistics and support costs. The 1970s-era Frigate Refit Complex in Devonport dockyard has since modernised and been transformed into a centre of excellence for the overhaul and upgrade of Type 23 frigates.

During their lives, the Type 23s have been progressively upgraded, with new weapons, sensors and other equipment being installed at regular intervals. The early ships of the class, which were laid down in the late 1980s, are starting to show their age and there is an urgent need to replace them when the new Type 26 frigates come online later this decade. Under current plans, however, the last Type 23, HMS *St Albans*, will not retire before 2035.

The latest iteration of the Type 23 upgrade programme is dubbed the Life Extension, or LIFEX, and it includes the installation of the Sea

Ceptor air defence missile to replace the old Sea Wolf weapons as well as a power generation machinery upgrade. The latter involves the replacement of four generators with more modern equipment to make the ships more efficient.

On cost grounds, the Royal Navy has not upgraded all its Type 23s to a common configuration. Until 2022 only eight of the class had received the latest generation Type 2087 towed

sonar array, but the whole fleet was equipped with the improved Type 997 Artisan 3D radar. As a result, the ships with the Type 2087 sonar are generally kept in European waters to counter Russian submarines, and ships without the new sonar have been deployed on more far-ranging missions to operational theatres with a less intense submarine threat.

In 2019, the first Type 23s started to receive the new Martlet close-in »

ABOVE: HMS *Argyll* in the Devonport Frigate Refit facility for a maintenance period in 2022. (BABCOCK)

BELOW: Type 23s are routinely deployed to participate in NATO exercises. (MOD/CROWN COPYRIGHT)

anti-ship missiles that are designed to counter swarms of fast patrol boats.

Three surplus Type 23s were sold to Chile, which is the only other operator of the ship, and delivered between 2006 and 2008.

In the 2021 Defence Review it was announced that two Type 23s would be retired early to save money on the cost of the LIFEX programme. HMS *Monmouth* was decommissioned in 2021 and HMS *Montrose* will follow in 2023.

TYPE 23 FRIGATE	
Builders: Yarrow Shipbuilders in Glasgow and Swan Hunter on Tyneside	
Cost: £135m per ship	
In commission: From November 1987	
Completed: 16	
Specifications	
Type: Anti-submarine warfare frigate	
Displacement: 4,900 tonnes (4,800 long tons)	
Length: 133m (436ft 4in)	
Beam: 16.1m (52ft 10in)	
Draught: 7.3m (23ft 11in)	
Propulsion: 2 × Rolls-Royce Marine Spey SM1C	
Speed: In excess of 28kts (52kph; 32mph)	
Range: 7,500nm (14,000km; 9,000 miles)	
Complement: 185 (accommodation for up to 205)	
Armament	
Anti-air missiles: 1 × 32-cell Sea Ceptor GWS 35 Vertical Launching System (VLS) canisters for 32 missiles (1–25+ km) replacing original Sea Wolf SAM	
Anti-ship Missiles: Up to 2 × quad Harpoon launchers (to be withdrawn by 2023)	
Anti-submarine torpedoes: 2 × twin 12.75in (324mm) Sting Ray torpedo tubes	
Guns: 1 × BAE 4.5in Mk 8 naval gun, 2 × 30mm DS30M Mk2 guns, or 2 × 30mm DS30B guns, 2 × Miniguns, 4 × 7.62mm General-Purpose Machine Guns	
Aviation facilities	
Flight deck and enclosed hangar	
Aircraft carried: 1 × Wildcat HMA2 or 1 × Merlin HM2	

HMS *Argyll*

HMS *Argyll* is the third ship of the Type 23 class but the oldest still in service. She was scheduled to be retired in 2023 but this date is likely to be extended because of delays to the new Type 26 class joining the fleet.

The ship has been highly active during her career, with her first major operation supporting the British intervention in Sierra Leone in 2000. This century she has seen extensive service in the Middle East, providing maritime security cover of Iraq and the wider region.

In 2017 the ship became the first Type 23 to receive the new Sea Ceptor air defence missile system as part of her Life Extension (LIFEX) and in 2022 she was dry docked for a further upgrade.

HMS *ARGYLL*	
Pennant number F231	
Ordered: September 1986	
Builder: Yarrow Shipbuilders on the Clyde, Glasgow	
Laid down: March 20, 1987	
Launched: April 8, 1989	
Commissioned: May 31, 1991	
Home port: HMNB Portsmouth	
Status: Post LIFEX upgrade	

HMS *Lancaster*

During her career HMS *Lancaster* has been involved in a wide range of duties, including counter-narcotics patrols in the Caribbean, NATO missions in European waters and counter-piracy operations off the coast of Somalia.

In 2015 she was the first Type 23 frigate to embark the new Wildcat HMA2 helicopter for an operational deployment. The Royal Navy placed the ship in extended readiness for two years ahead of a major Life Extension (LIFEX) upgrade that installed the Artisan 3D radar, Sea Ceptor air defence missiles and made other improvements.

HMS *Lancaster* returned to service in 2020 but has since been earmarked to deploy to Bahrain later in 2022 to replace HMS *Montrose* as the Royal Navy's forward-deployed asset. During her time in the Gulf fresh crews will be rotated through duty on the ship. Ahead of her deployment the ship received a full complement of eight Harpoon anti-ship missiles. »

HMS *LANCASTER*	
Pennant number F229	
Ordered: September 1986	
Builder: Yarrow Shipbuilders on the Clyde, Glasgow	
Laid down: December 18, 1987	
Launched: May 24, 1990	
Commissioned: May 1, 1992	
Home port: HMNB Portsmouth	
Status: Active service	

LEFT: HMS *Argyll* underwent her post Life Extension overhaul in Devonport dockyard during 2017. (BABCOCK)

BELOW: HMS *Lancaster* will take over from HMS *Montrose* on Gulf duty in 2023. (MOD/CROWN COPYRIGHT)

ABOVE: HMS *Iron Duke* on a counter-piracy patrol off Somalia. (MOD/CROWN COPYRIGHT)

HMS *Iron Duke*

The ship is named after victor of the Battle of Waterloo, the Duke of Wellington, who was nicknamed the Iron Duke.

HMS *Iron Duke* was part of the naval task force that supported the British intervention in Sierra Leone in 2000. In 2011 she fired her 4.5in gun in anger to bombard Libyan troops fighting rebel forces near the town of Misrata.

Her systems have been progressively upgraded, with the Artisan 3D radar being installed in 2012-13. In 2017 she was laid up for two years because of

HMS *IRON DUKE*
Pennant number F234
Ordered: July 1988
Builder: Yarrow Shipbuilders on the Clyde, Glasgow
Laid down: December 12, 1988
Launched: March 2, 1991
Commissioned: May 20, 1993
Home port: HMNB Portsmouth
Status: In LIFEX

a shortage of sailors across the fleet and then entered a Life Extension upgrade to install the new Sea Ceptor air defence mission system.

HMS *Montrose*

During the 1990s HMS *Montrose* deployed twice to the Falkland Islands as the South Atlantic guard ship. She took part in maritime security

RIGHT: HMS *Montrose* has been forward-deployed in the Arabian Gulf since 2019. (MOD/CROWN COPYRIGHT)

operations off the coast of Iraq in 2006 and the following year supported NATO operations in the Mediterranean before returning to the Gulf region. In 2010 her Lynx helicopter destroyed a pirate craft off the coast of Somalia.

Between 2014 and 2017 the ship underwent a Life Extension upgrade to install the Sea Ceptor air defence missile system. In 2019 she was forward-based in Bahrain in the Arabian Gulf for a four-year period during which her crew was to be rotated. This new method of crewing saves on sailing time back and forth to the UK. Soon after arriving in the Gulf HMS *Montrose* was involved in a standoff with Iranian naval forces

that were threatening British-flagged merchant shipping in the Strait of Hormuz. She is due to return home in 2023, ahead of her retirement.

HMS *MONTROSE*
Pennant number F236
Ordered: July 1988
Builder: Yarrow Shipbuilders on the Clyde, Glasgow
Laid down: November 1, 1989
Launched: July 31, 1992
Commissioned: June 2, 1994
Home port: HMS Jufair, Bahrain
Status: Active service

HMS *Westminster*

Soon after joining the fleet HMS *Westminster* was deployed to the Caribbean on counter-drugs operations but was quickly re-tasked to provide humanitarian assistance after the island of Montserrat was devastated by a volcanic eruption in 1995.

In 2004 the ship was the first Type 23 frigate to embark a Merlin HM2 for an operational deployment. Later that year she also received the Type 2087 towed-sonar array in a significant upgrade to her anti-submarine capabilities.

HMS *Westminster* joined the international naval forces blockading Libya during the NATO intervention in support of rebel forces in the North African country in 2011. Her advanced anti-submarine warfare capabilities have meant HMS *Westminster* has been used extensively during NATO exercises in the North Atlantic and Mediterranean.

In 2014 she docked at Portsmouth naval base to begin a three-year Life Extension refit, including the installation of the Sea Ceptor air defence missile system.

HMS *WESTMINSTER*
Pennant number F237
Ordered: December 1989
Builder: Swan Hunter, Tyne and Wear
Laid down: January 18, 1991
Launched: February 4, 1992
Commissioned: May 13, 1994
Home port: HMNB Portsmouth
Status: Active service

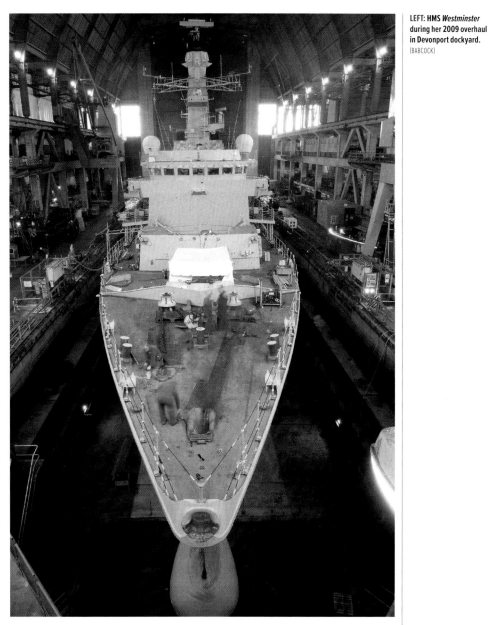

LEFT: **HMS** *Westminster* during her 2009 overhaul in Devonport dockyard. (BABCOCK)

HMS *Northumberland*

On her maiden cruise to the Falkland Islands, HMS *Northumberland* suffered major storm damage to her bow and subsequently had to go into a Brazilian dry dock to be repaired.

From 2004 to 2005 the ship received a major upgrade to install the Type 2087 towed-sonar array and modifications to her hangar and flight deck to accommodate Merlin anti-submarine helicopters.

She was the first Royal Navy warship to participate in the European Union anti-piracy mission off Somalia in 2008 and returned to the region again in 2010.

In 2016 she began a two-year Life Extension upgrade to install the Sea Ceptor air defence missile system. While on a mission to track a Russian submarine in the North Atlantic her towed sonar was damaged after contact with the Russian vessel. »

HMS *NORTHUMBERLAND*
Pennant number F238
Ordered: December 1989
Builder: Swan Hunter, Tyne and Wear
Laid down: April 4, 1991
Launched: April 4, 1992
Commissioned: September 29, 1994
Home port: HMNB Devonport, Plymouth
Status: Active service

LEFT: **HMS** *Northumberland* on deployment in the Indian Ocean. (MOD/CROWN COPYRIGHT)

HMS *Richmond*

Her first major deployment was to the Far East in 1997 as part of the Ocean Wave 97 Task Group. The ship's combat operation was as part of the naval task force supporting the amphibious landing by Royal Marines on the al-Faw peninsula in southern Iraq in March 2003. In the opening hours of the landings, HMS *Richmond* provided naval gunfire support for Royal Marines fighting ashore.

The ship received Sea Ceptor air defence missiles and new MTU M53B diesel generators during a Life Extension upgrade between 2018

HMS *RICHMOND*
Pennant number F239
Ordered: December 1989
Builder: Swan Hunter, Tyne and Wear
Laid down: February 16, 1992
Launched: April 6, 1993
Commissioned: June 22,1995
Home port: HMNB Devonport, Plymouth
Status: Active service

and 2020. Previously she had been fitted with the Type 2087 towed-sonar array. The following year she joined HMS *Queen Elizabeth* as part of the

Carrier Strike Group 21 deployment to the Far East.

HMS *Somerset*

During her career HMS *Somerset* has been very active in support of UK forces and allied operations. She hosted peace talks off Sierra Leone in 1991 and in 2009 joined an amphibious task force to the Far East, led by the helicopter carrier HMS *Ocean*. The following year the ship joined coalition maritime security operations off Iraq's coast.

In 2015 she joined forces with the UK Border Force to intercept and arrest a Tanzanian-registered tugboat 100 miles off Aberdeen. More than three tons of cocaine was found aboard the vessel.

She has received several major upgrades, including 30mm automated cannon turrets and Type 2087 towed-sonar array in 2007 and in 2018 the ship began a four-year Life Extension period that included the installation of the Sea Ceptor air defence missile systems to replace her old Sea Wolf system.

HMS *SOMERSET*
Pennant number F82
Ordered: January 1992
Builder: Marconi Marine, Glasgow
Laid down: October 12, 1992
Launched: June 25, 1994
Commissioned: September 20, 1996
Home port: HMNB Devonport, Plymouth
Status: Active service

HMS *Sutherland*

The ship's first major operation was during the 2011 Libyan crisis when she was part of the Royal Navy task force headed by the helicopter carrier HMS *Ocean*. After one stint patrolling off Libya, HMS *Sutherland* withdrew to re-stock her stores from the NATO naval base at Souda Bay on Crete. The ship then returned to help support HMS *Ocean* as she launched Army Air Corps Apache AH1 attack helicopters to raid the Libyan coast.

In 2019 the ship was used to evaluate the installation of Martlet anti-ship

regime she returned to the region in 2006 to mount patrols to protect Iraq's off-shore oil export infrastructure.

She conducted anti-piracy patrols off Somalia in 2013 and then again in 2014. In 2016 HMS *Kent* began a two-year Life Extension upgrade period, during which she was equipped with the new Sea Ceptor missile systems. Previously she had been fitted with the Type 2087 towed-sonar array.

The ship accompanied HMS *Queen Elizabeth* to the Far East in 2021 as part of the Carrier Strike Group 21 deployment. »

HMS *KENT*	
Pennant number F78	
Ordered: February 1996	
Builder: Marconi Marine, Glasgow	
Laid down: April 16, 1997	
Launched: May 27, 1998	
Commissioned: June 8, 2000	
Home port: HMNB Devonport, Plymouth	
Status: Active service	

ABOVE: HMS *Sutherland* is now undergoing a Life Extension and overhaul in Devonport dockyard.
(MOD/CROWN COPYRIGHT)

BELOW: HMS *Kent* during an anti-piracy patrol off Somalia in 2015.
(MOD/CROWN COPYRIGHT)

HMS *SUTHERLAND*	
Pennant number F81	
Ordered: January 1992	
Builder: Marconi Marine, Glasgow	
Laid down: October 14, 1993	
Launched: March 9, 1996	
Commissioned: July 4, 1997	
Home port: HMNB Devonport, Plymouth	
Status: In LIFEX	

missiles to boost its defences against swarms of hostile small gun boats. In 2021 she began a four-year Life Extension refit to install the Sea Ceptor air defence missile systems and other improvements. Previously she had been fitted with the Type 2087 towed-sonar array.

HMS *Kent*

HMS *Kent* was heavily involved in maritime security operations in the northern Arabian Gulf, including enforcing UN sanctions on Iraq in 2002. After the fall of Saddam Hussein's

ABOVE: HMS *Portland* off Devonport naval base. (MOD/CROWN COPYRIGHT)

HMS *Portland*

HMS *Portland* holds the speed record for Royal Navy Type 23 frigates after recording 30.8 knots, or 57kph, during her sea trials in 2000.

Tragedy struck the ship in December 2014 when her Lynx was involved in an accident and the helicopter's four crew were killed.

In 2007 she took part in a counter-drug operation alongside the US Coast Guard and seized a vessel in the Caribbean that was found to be carry 3.5 tonnes of cocaine.

HMS PORTLAND	
Pennant number F79	
Ordered: February 1996	
Builder: Marconi Marine, Glasgow	
Laid down: January 14, 1998	
Launched: May 15, 1999	
Commissioned: May 3, 2001	
Home port: HMNB Devonport, Plymouth	
Status: Active service	

An upgrade in 2012 installed the 2087 towed-sonar array and made other improvements. This was followed by a further Life Extension upgrade period between 2018 and 2021 involving the fitting of Sea Ceptor air defence missiles, a Type 997 surveillance radar and Type 2150 hull-mounted sonar.

HMS *St Albans*

As the 16th and final Type 23 to be built, HMS *St Albans* is expected to

RIGHT: HMS *St Albans* on exercise in the India Ocean with HMS *Argyll*. (MOD/CROWN COPYRIGHT)

HMS ST ALBANS	
Pennant number F83	
Ordered: February 1996	
Builder: Marconi Marine, Glasgow	
Laid down: April 18, 1999	
Launched: May 6, 2000	
Commissioned: June 6, 2002	
Home port: HMNB Devonport, Plymouth	
Status: In LIFEX	

be the last to be retired, with her out-of-service date currently projected as 2035.

The ship has seen extensive service in Middle East waters, including maritime security duties in the Gulf region in 2004 and 2006. During the cruise home from that later deployment, she was diverted to assist in the evacuation of British nationals from Lebanon, under Operation Highbrow. This included making runs to the port of Beirut to bring out British citizens.

Upgrades including the installation of the Type 2087 towed-sonar array and the conversion of her hangar and flight deck to accommodate Merlin anti-submarine helicopters took place in 2007-08. An all-electric 4.5in Mod1 gun was installed in 2014. Sea Ceptor is currently being installed during a Life Extension period that began in 2019.

The Mine Countermeasures Force

Keeping the Sea Lanes Open

Sandown-class Mine Hunters

The Sandown-class Mine Countermeasure Vessels are all based in Scotland as part of the 1st Mine Countermeasures (MCM1) Squadron. They routinely deploy to the Northern Gulf, conduct exercises with other NATO nations and work around the British coastline. As well as preparing for combat operations, the vessels and their crews are often involved in clearing old ordnance, the legacy of previous wars.

The vessels have glass-reinforced plastic hulls to allow them to operate in close proximity to magnetic sea mines. Their role is to clear mines to allow safe passage for larger forces, detecting and destroying any hidden dangers swiftly.

They are protected by a single 30mm DS30M Mark 2 cannon, controlled from a remote-operator console elsewhere on the ship. The ships are equipped with the SeaFox Mine Disposal System, which comprises a

LEFT: Sandown-class mine countermeasure vessels are all set to be retired by 2025. (MOD/CROWNCOPYRIGHT)

remotely operated submersible that is used to identify underwater explosives and mines. It is controlled via fibre optic cables from the parent ship. Once a mine has been found, another SeaFox unit is guided to the target to place a shaped charge next to it. The resulting explosion usually neutralises the threat.

The 2021 Defence White Paper announced that all mine countermeasure vessels in the Royal Navy would be retired during the 2020s to be replaced by automated systems. All the remaining Sandown-class ships are therefore scheduled to be retired by 2025.

In June 2021 it was announced that two Sandown-class ships were to be transferred to the Ukrainian Navy

upon decommissioning. HMS *Ramsey* and HMS *Blyth* were decommissioned in August 2021 to allow them to be refitted by Babcock ahead of their transfer to the Ukrainian Navy. »

SANDOWN-CLASS MINE HUNTERS

Name	Pennant number
HMS *Penzance*	M106
HMS *Pembroke*	M107
HMS *Grimsby*	M108
HMS *Bangor*	M109
HMS *Shoreham*	M112
Decommissioned, awaiting transfer to Ukrainian Navy	
HMS *Ramsey*	M110
HMS *Blyth*	M111

SANDOWN CLASS

Builders: Vosper Thornycroft, Woolston, Hampshire	
In service: 1989	
Completed: 15	
Active: 11 (5 Royal Navy, 3 each Estonian and Royal Saudi Navies)	
Specifications	
Displacement: 600 tons	
Length: 52.5m (172ft 3in)	
Beam: 10.9m (35ft 9in)	
Draught: 2.3m (7ft 7in)	
Propulsion	
Paxman Valenta 6RP200E diesels	
Speed: 13kts (24kph; 15mph)	
Complement: 34 (accommodation for up to 40)	
Sensors	
Sonar Type 2093	
SeaFox mine disposal system	
Diver-placed explosive charges	
Armament	
1 × 30mm DS30M Mark 2 Automated Small Calibre Gun, 3 × Miniguns	
2 × General Purpose Machine Guns	

LEFT: 30mm DS30M Mark 2 cannon protect Royal Navy's Sandown-class mine countermeasure vessels. (MOD/CROWNCOPYRIGHT)

Hunt-Class Mine Countermeasure Vessels

When the first of the 13 Hunt class were introduced in the 1980s, they were the largest warships ever built out of glass-reinforced plastic and the last in operation to use the Napier Deltic diesel engine. Vosper Thornycroft in Woolston, Hampshire, built 11 of the ships and the remaining two were built by Yarrow Shipbuilders on the River Clyde at Glasgow.

BAE Systems re-engined the last eight Royal Navy vessels with new Caterpillar CAT C32 engines, together with new gearboxes, bow thrusters, propellers, and control systems. A further refurbishment programme ran from 2012 to 2018.

The remaining eight vessels have had Type 2193 sonar and the NAUTIS 3 command systems installed. The sonar is capable of detecting and classifying an object the size of a football at a distance of up to 1,000 metres. The SeaFox Mine Disposal System is used from the vessels. The Royal Navy announced that all the vessels would be withdrawn from service by 2031, to be replaced by autonomous systems.

Name	Pennant number
HMS *Ledbury*	M30
HMS *Cattistock*	M31
HMS *Brocklesby*	M33
HMS *Middleton*	M34
HMS *Chiddingfold*	M37
HMS *Hurworth*	M39

All the ships of the class are currently operated by the 2nd Mine Countermeasures (MCM2) Squadron, which is home ported at HMNB Portsmouth.

HUNT CLASS

Builders: Vosper Thornycroft and Yarrow Shipbuilders Limited	
Built: 1978–1988	
In commission: 1979–present	
Completed: 13	
Active: 10 (6 Royal Navy, 1 Greek Navy, 3 Lithuanian Naval Force)	
Specifications	
Displacement: 750 tons	
Length: 60m (196ft 10in)	
Beam: 9.8m (32ft 2in)	
Draught: 2.2m (7ft 3in)	
Propulsion: 2 shaft CAT C32 diesel	
Complement: 45 (6 officers and 39 ratings)	
Sensors	
Sonar Type 2193	
SeaFox mine disposal system	
Armament	
1 × 30mm DS30M Mark 2, 2 × Miniguns, 3 × General Purpose Machine guns	

Mine-Hunting Capability (MHC) Programme

This is a major project to replace all the Royal Navy's existing mine countermeasure (MCM) vessels. The first 'block' of this work has already been contracted under the banner of the UK-France Maritime Mine Countermeasures (MMCM) programme. Three mission systems, usually classed as a control hub, autonomous launch platforms for several unmanned underwater vehicles (UUVs) or unmanned surface vehicles (USVs) and maintenance

facilities, are expected to be delivered by the mid-2020s to replace the six Sandown-class MCMs. MHC Block 2 will replace the last six Hunt-class vessels by 2030. A potential budget of £1 billion is available.

MHC Block 1 and Block 2 unmanned systems are first expected to be deployed from existing in-service Bay-class or Albion-class amphibious landing ships. They would then migrate onto the new Multi-Role Support Ship or frigates, with MCM systems inserted as modules in mission bays.

Atlas Elektronik UK manufactures the ATLAS Remote Combined Influence Minesweeping System (ARCIMS). A £25 million contract was awarded in early 2021 for the supply of three combined influence minesweeping systems. Trials and training are underway at the Royal Navy's Maritime Autonomous System Trials Team (MASTT) organisation, ahead of entry to service in 2022. Sweep systems such as this are intended to rapidly clear safe routes through known mine fields.

The UK-based autonomous Route Survey (RTSV) capability is operating under the title of Project Wilton. It is initially being deployed at the Faslane Naval Base in Scotland, but the system is road-transportable and able to cover the whole of Scotland and the north of England. RTSV involves regular detailed mapping of the seabed so that any newly laid object can be spotted and investigated quickly. The approaches to the River Clyde are especially sensitive, as this is the entry and exit route for the UK nuclear deterrent submarines. The Wilton team are equipped with three boats that can carry off-the-shelf REMUS 100 and 600 small-medium UUVs, side-scan sonar and M500 UUV. AEUK is the prime contractor on the programme and supplies the SEA boat platforms.

LEFT: Fleet divers will soon no longer have to conduct dangerous missions to inspect underwater mine threats. (MOD/CROWNCOPYRIGHT)

BELOW: The ATLAS Remote Combined Influence Minesweeping System (ARCIMS) is the Royal Navy's first fully robotic mine hunting system. (ATLAS ELEKTRONIK)

Patrol and Survey Vessels

On Watch Around the Globe

ABOVE: HMS *Severn*, HMS *Tyne* and HMS *Mersey* exercising off the coast of Cornwall in 2012. (MOD/CROWN COPYRIGHT)

Royal Navy River-class Offshore Patrol Vessels protect the UK's interests at home and abroad, safeguarding territorial waters, protecting fishing stocks, performing constabulary duties and acting as the eyes and ears of the fleet.

The ships were bought in two batches, with the most recent order for five vessels having been placed in 2016. The ships are designed to operate in home waters as well as further afield, fulfilling overseas forward-presence roles to allow the release of Type 23 frigates for duties more suited to a higher-capability warship.

Batch 2 vessels are bigger and more capable than the first three ships. Each ship has 30mm guns as its main armament, controlled from a remote-operator console elsewhere on the ship.

HMS *Tyne,* HMS *Severn,* and HMS *Mersey* belong to the first batch, built by Vosper Thornycroft, and they have been in service since the early 2000s. All the ships of the second batch were constructed at BAE Systems' Govan shipyard, then transferred to the company's Scotstoun shipyard

RIVER-CLASS PATROL VESSEL

Name	Pennant number
Batch 1	
HMS *Tyne*	P281
HMS *Severn*	P282
HMS *Mersey*	P283
Batch 2	
HMS *Forth*	P222
HMS *Medway*	P223
HMS *Trent*	P224
HMS *Tamar*	P233
HMS *Spey*	P234

RIVER-CLASS OFFSHORE PATROL VESSEL

Builders:	
Batch 1 – Vosper Thornycroft	
Batch 2 – BAE Systems Maritime – Naval Ships	
Built: 2001–present	
In commission: 2003–present	
Active: 8	
Specifications	
Displacement:	
Batch 1 – 1,700 tons	
Batch 2 – 2,000 tons	
Length:	
Batch 1 – 79.5m (260ft 10in)	
Batch 2 – 90.5m (296ft 11in)	
Beam:	
Batch 1 – 13.5m (44ft 3in)	
Batch 2 – 13.5m (44ft 3in)	
Draught:	
Batch 1 – 3.8m (12ft 6in)	
Speed:Batch 1 – 20kts (37kph; 23mph)	
Batch 2 – 25kts (46kph; 29mph)	
Range:	
Batch 1 – 5,500nm (10,200km; 6,300 miles)	
Batch 2 – 5,500nm (10,200km; 6,300 miles)	
Armament	
Batch 1 – 1 × Oerlikon 20mm cannon, 2 × General Purpose Machine Guns	
Batch 2 – 1 × Bushmaster 30mm cannon, 2 × Miniguns, 2 × General Purpose Machine Guns	
Aviation facilities	
Batch 2 – Merlin-capable flight deck	

for fitting out. The eight River-class vessels are based in, and crewed from, Portsmouth as part of the Overseas Patrol Squadron.

In an emergency the Royal Navy might have to attach anti-ship missiles to its Batch 2 River-class patrol ships to make up for its lack of surface warfare frigates and destroyers, and additional upgrades could include attaching a Bofors 57mm gun. However, this upgrade had not yet been approved.

On September 7, 2021 both HMS *Spey* and HMS *Tamar* left Portsmouth to be forward-deployed to the Indo-Pacific region. It is anticipated that they will not return for a minimum of five years and could stay in the region for up to 10 years.

RIGHT: HMS *Tamar*, a Batch 2 River-class vessel heads up the Thames past the Canary Wharf complex. (NICKNOMI)

Other Patrol Vessels

ABOVE LEFT AND ABOVE RIGHT: HMS *Protector* is the Royal Navy's dedicated ice patrol ship. It operates predominately in the Antarctic region and off the Falkland Islands conducting scientific research and maintaining a British presence in the South Atlantic. She was originally a commercial vessel that was chartered by the Ministry of Defence in 2011. Two years later she was purchased outright for the Royal Navy. (MOD/CROWN COPYRIGHT)

LEFT: HMS *Raider* is one of 16 Archer- or P2000-class patrol vessels that operate in the fisher protection, counter-migrant and port security roles. The Coastal Forces Squadron has 12 of the vessels, which are also assigned to support University Naval Squadrons. Two boats each also serve with the Faslane Patrol Boat Squadron and the Gibraltar Patrol Boat Squadron. (MOD/CROWN COPYRIGHT)

FAR LEFT: HMS *Echo* is one of four dedicated oceanographic survey vessels operated by the Royal Navy to map the sea bed. Her sister ship, HMS *Enterprise* is also a multi-role vessel, operating in coastal regions around the world. HMS *Scott* has an ocean surveying role. The small HMS *Magpie* operates in UK waters. (MOD/CROWN COPYRIGHT)

LEFT: The Archer-class patrol boat, HMS *Dasher*, at speed off Faslane where she provides maritime security for the home of the UK's nuclear deterrent. (MOD/CROWN COPYRIGHT)

The Royal Fleet Auxiliary

Supporting the Fleet

The Royal Fleet Auxiliary, or RFA, is a Merchant Navy organisation that is made up of nine civilian-crewed ships operated by the Ministry of Defence. It provides vital – and highly valued – logistical and operational support to the Royal Navy and Royal Marines, as well as other branches of the British Armed Forces.

It is formally part of Britain's Naval Service, and the RFA's personnel wear Royal Navy uniforms complemented by Merchant Navy-styled insignia. As a result, its personnel are governed by a mixture of Merchant Navy, Civil Service and Naval discipline regulations. Although nominally civilians, RFA personnel are all Naval Reservists who can be rapidly mobilised in time of conflict. RFA personnel are trained at Royal Navy establishments but are not routinely armed or trained to operate weapon systems installed in their ships. The crews of RFA vessels are augmented by Royal Navy sailors who operate specialist communications systems, electronic countermeasures and defensive weapons. They are also assigned to embarked aviation detachments.

The RFA was formed in 1905, as the Royal Navy started to set up a global network of coaling stations to fuel the steam-driven battleships of that era. Once the Royal Navy had transitioned to oil-powered warships the RFA had to change to supply this new form of fuel as well as food, water, and other essential supplies.

The modern RFA came into its own in World War Two when the Royal Navy developed new concepts to supply large naval task forces

operating far out at sea. These freed the Royal Navy from dependence on shore bases to re-supply its fleets and meant large naval forces could operate independently for long periods. This was particularly important in the protection of supply convoys in the North Atlantic and in aircraft carrier operations in the Pacific against the Japanese.

New techniques to transfer fuel, oil, and other supplies to warships underway at sea were developed. Known as Replenishment At Sea, or RAS, these involved the development of specialist equipment including cranes and hoists to move pallets of stores from supply ships to warships while both ships were moving at speed. Perhaps the most significant RAS equipment to be developed were extendable pipes that could be passed from oil tankers to warships to refuel them.

The modern RFA operates supply ships and tankers with the current generations of RAS equipment installed to sustain Royal Navy ships far from home. Some 1,800 personnel currently serve in the RFA.

As well as its traditional at sea logistic support role, the modern RFA also operates many other types of support vessels for the Royal Navy. The three Bay-class amphibious landing ships support the Royal Marines and function as 'mother ships' for mine countermeasure task

forces. It also operates the aviation support ship RFA *Argus*, which can also be re-roled as a hospital ship, or Primary Casualty Receiving Ship (PCRS) as it is known. In 2014 that ship was dispatched to Sierra Leone to provide medical support to counter the outbreak of the deadly Ebola virus.

The RFA headquarters is in Portsmouth and its ships are based

in the main Royal Navy bases at Devonport, the Marchwood military port in Hampshire and Falmouth Harbour in Cornwall. A&P Group's Falmouth shipyard maintains and supports the Bay-class landing ships and the Cammell Laird shipyard in Birkenhead in Merseyside has a long-term support contract for the other main RFA vessels.

ABOVE: Sailors on HMS *Dragon* prepare to receive stores from a Royal Fleet Auxiliary ship. (MOD/CROWN COPYRIGHT)

BELOW: RFA *Tidesurge* passes fuel to HMS *Prince of Wales* during a NATO exercise in the Norwegian Sea. (MOD/CROWN COPYRIGHT)

Bay-class Landing Ships

Landing the Royal Marines

RIGHT: RFA *Mounts Bay* seen from above as the ship's company parade on her flight deck in honour of the late Queen's Platinum Jubilee.
(MOD/CROWN COPYRIGHT)

BAY-CLASS LANDING SHIP DOCK	
Builders: Swan Hunter and BAE Systems Naval Ships	
Cost: £596m for 4 units	
Built: January 2002-November 2007	
In commission: July 2006-present	
Completed: 4	
Specifications	
Displacement: 16,160 tonnes (15,900 long tons)	
Length: 176.6m (579.4ft)	
Beam: 26.4m (86.6ft)	
Draught: 5.8m (19ft)	
Speed: 18kts (33kph; 21mph)	
Range: 8,000nm (15,000km; 9,200 miles)	
Boats & landing craft carried: 1 × LCU or 2 × LCVP in well dock, 2 × Mexeflote powered rafts	
Complement: 70 (RFA core crew)	
Capacity: 1,150 linear metres of vehicles (up to 24 Challenger 2 tanks or 150 light trucks) Cargo capacity of 200 tons ammunition or 24 TEU containers	
Troops: 356 (standard), 700 (overload)	
Armament	
Fitted for: 2 × 30mm DS30B cannon, 2 × Phalanx CIWS, 4 × 7.62mm Mk44 Miniguns, 6 × 7.62mm L7 General Purpose Machine Guns	
Aviation facilities: Flight deck for helicopters up to Chinook-size; temporary hangar can be fitted	

The three Bay-class Landing Ship Docks (LSDs) are considered the most versatile ships in the Royal Fleet Auxiliary. They were purchased to replace the old Knights of the Round Table-class landing ships that provided sterling service for nearly 40 years. The images of the RFA *Sir Galahad* on fire at Bluff Cove in the Falklands conflict in 1982 made the landing ship iconic. They were considered an essential component of the Royal Navy's amphibious shipping flotilla in supporting the Royal Marines. When not participating in amphibious exercises or operations, the landing ships moved dangerous stores such as artillery ammunition and missiles between the UK and overseas British Army garrisons.

So, in the late 1990s, when plans for a replacement were being developed, there was strong support across the Ministry of Defence, Royal Navy, and Royal Marines. With some modifications, the existing Dutch-Spanish Royal Schelde's Enforcer design was selected to be basis for the new Bay-class vessels.

This design features a large well dock that can accommodate two landing craft and two Mexeflote ferries. There is an internal ramp to allow the landing craft or ferries to be loaded into the vessel at sea. The ships also have steerable azimuth thrusters which allow them to be manoeuvred into small harbours or close to shorelines. The rear ramp can be used to load vehicles from quaysides or

RIGHT: The Bay-class landing ships have a very distinctive forward profile.
(MOD/CROWN COPYRIGHT)

LEFT: Royal Marines prepare to launch raiding craft from the well dock of RFA *Mounts Bay*. (MOD/CROWN COPYRIGHT)

at commercial ferry terminals. Two 30-ton capacity cranes can lift ISO containers onto the deck without the need for shore-based loading systems.

Unlike the Dutch versions, however, the British Bay class does not have an enclosed hanger to support aviation operations, although the flight deck can accommodate several helicopters, including the big Chinook.

The construction of the vessels ran into trouble very quickly after the Ministry of Defence split the order to ensure that shipyards in both Glasgow and the northeast of England received orders for two ships each. Swan Hunter, located on Tyneside, fell behind schedule and claimed it needed additional funds to complete the work. Eventually, the Ministry of Defence lost patience with Swan

Hunter and in 2006 ordered them to stop work. The unfinished hulls were moved to BAE Systems' yard at Govan to be completed. It had been envisaged that each company would be paid no more than £122m for their two ships but the four ships ended up costing £596m in total.

Nevertheless, the four ships proved to be highly effective vessels after they entered service, beginning in 2006. Only four years later the new Conservative-led coalition government ordered a round of defence cuts, including a reduction in the amphibious shipping fleet. One of the Bay-class LSDs was sold off and ended up in the Royal Australian Navy as HMAS *Choules*.

In RFA service the remaining three Bay-class vessels have been highly active

in many roles, including providing humanitarian relief in the Caribbean, hosting training for the Iraqi Navy and providing a mothership capability for Royal Navy mine countermeasure vessels in the Arabian Gulf. More recently they have been used as trials vessels to host unmanned craft.

The ships are now playing a key role in the development of the Littoral Strike Group's concept and are playing host to detachments of Royal Marines equipped with raiding craft, attack helicopters and unmanned aerial vehicles. Eventually the Royal Navy intends to buy purpose-built Littoral Strike Ships but project has been delayed until after 2030, so the Bay class will have a role to play in Littoral Strike operations by the Royal Marines until then. »

BELOW: RFA *Cardigan Bay* docked in the Italian port of La Spézia in 2007. (LUDOVIC PÉRON)

ABOVE: RFA *Lyme Bay* under construction on the River Clyde in Glasgow. (SIMON JOHNSTON, GOVAN SHIPBUILDERS)

RIGHT: RFA *Cardigan Bay* has conducted extended periods of duty in the Arabian Gulf. (MOD/CROWN COPYRIGHT)

RFA *Lyme Bay*

RFA *Lyme Bay* joined the fleet in 2007 and two years later was deployed to Bahrain to become the 'mothership' to the Royal Navy Mine Countermeasures Group operating in the Arabian Gulf. She remained on station for three years until returning home to the UK for regeneration.

In 2013 she was dispatched to the Indian Ocean to participate in counter-piracy missions off the coast of Somalia, hosting Royal Marine boarding parties. For six months in 2015 she deployed to the Caribbean on Hurricane Watch and eventually supported relief operations on Dominica and The Bahamas. In 2021 she returned to the Gulf to support mine countermeasure operations.

RFA *LYME BAY*	
Pennant number L3007	
Ordered: December 18, 2000	
Builder: Swan Hunter and BAE Systems	
Laid down: November 22, 2002	
Launched: September 3, 2005	
In service: November 26, 2007	
Home port: Falmouth	
Status: Active service	

RFA *Mounts Bay*

The ship has predominately been employed in the amphibious role, supporting Royal Marines' landing exercises in the UK, Europe and further afield. Major exercises have included Exercise Clockwork in north Norway in 2006, the Vela deployment to Sierra Leone in the same year, and the Joint Warrior training exercises off Scotland in 2008.

In 2016, she deployed to the Aegean Sea to help in operations in response to migrant crossings into Greece from Turkey and then took part in European Union operations off Libya to intercept migrants heading to Italy. She conducted humanitarian relief operations in The Bahamas in 2019

RIGHT: RFA *Mounts Bay* in BAE Systems' yard on the River Clyde in Glasgow in 2004. (ALF VAN BEEM)

RFA *MOUNTS BAY*	
Pennant number L3008	
Ordered: November 19, 2001	
Builder: BAE Systems, Govan, Glasgow	
Laid down: August 25, 2002	
Launched: April 9, 2004	
In service: July 13, 2006	
Home port: Falmouth	
Status: Active service	

and in 2022 joined the major NATO exercise in the Arctic circle, dubbed Cold Response.

RFA *Cardigan Bay*

RFA *Cardigan Bay* has spent extended periods of her career operating in the Indian Ocean and Arabian Gulf regions.

In 2011 she was part of the Royal Navy Response Force deployment to the Mediterranean and Indian Ocean, with personnel of 40 Commando Royal Marines embarked. During this cruise

she was diverted to Yemen to stand ready to evacuate British nationals after unrest gripped the country. Later in the deployment her Royal Marines landed in Somaliland to train local forces in counter-piracy operations.

The ship was deployed to Bahrain in 2017 to begin a four-year period as the mothership for the UK Mine Countermeasures Group in the Arabian Gulf. She was relieved by RFA *Lyme Bay* in May 2021, which allowed her to return to the UK for a refit. She is expected to return to Gulf duty in the near future.

RFA *CARDIGAN BAY*	
Pennant number L3009	
Ordered: November 19, 2001	
Builder: BAE Systems, Govan, Glasgow	
Laid down: October 13, 2003	
Launched: April 8-9, 2005	
In service: December 18, 2006	
Home port: Falmouth	
Status: Active service	

Tide-class Fast Fleet Tanker

Keeping the Fleet Ready for Action

The four Tide-class Fast Fleet Tankers are the Royal Fleet Auxiliary's newest ships and entered service from 2017. They were the result of the Military Afloat Reach and Sustainability (MARS) project, which aimed to replace the old Leaf and Rover-class fleet tankers.

In 2012, the Ministry of Defence contracted Daewoo Shipbuilding & Marine Engineering (DSME) of South Korea to build the four hulls for £452 million. The final fitting out of the ships with sensitive UK military items took place at A&P Group's yard in Falmouth, Cornwall, and involved several British companies, under contracts worth around £150m.

The ships were a derivative of BMT Defence Services' AEGIR-26 design, which in turn evolved from a civilian tanker design. They were built with a double hull to reduce oil being lost in the event of damage to the outer hull, in line with the civilian maritime regulations. The RFA's older tankers conformed to military specifications and had only single hulls, which meant many ports around the world would not allow them to dock.

Royal Navy commanders wanted the new tankers to support long-range missions by the new Queen Elizabeth-

class aircraft carriers. Without reliable logistic support, the new aircraft carriers were limited to operations close to their home bases.

The ships were designed with three stations to conduct replenishment at sea (RAS) while cruising abeam of the aircraft carriers and other warships. They have the ability to carry and pass diesel oil, aviation fuel and fresh water. There is also a rig for astern replenishment operations.

The Tide class has a flight deck and helicopter hangar to allow vertical RAS, with the capacity to carry Chinook-sized helicopters. Propulsion is via medium-speed diesel engines driving twin shafts in

a hybrid Combined Diesel-electric or Diesel (CODELOD) arrangement. This is designed for fuel efficiency across a wide range of speeds. »

LEFT: RFA *Tidespring* conducts a dual replenishment at sea with **HMS** *Lancaster* and **HMS** *Westminster*. (MOD/CROWN COPYRIGHT)

TIDE CLASS FAST FLEET TANKER

Builders: DSME, South Korea	
Cost: £452m (eventually £550m for four vessels)	
In service: 2017-present	
Active: 4	
Specifications	
Displacement: 39,000 tons	
Length: 200.9m (659ft 1in)	
Beam: 28.6m (93ft 10in)	
Draft: 10m (32ft 10in)	
Propulsion: CODELOD	
Speed: 20kts (37kph; 23mph)	
Range: 18,200nm (33,700km; 20,900 miles)	
Complement: 63 plus 46 non-crew embarked persons (Royal Marines, flight crew, trainees)	
Capacity	
Tanks for diesel oil, aviation fuel and fresh water	
Stowage for up to 8 × 20 containers	
Armament	
2 × Phalanx CIWS (fitted for but not with, depending on deployment), 2 × 30mm cannons	
Aviation facilities	
Enclosed Merlin capable hangar	
Large Chinook capable flight deck	
Aircraft carried: 1 x Wildcat or Merlin	

LEFT: RFA *Tidespring* during Exercise Strike Warrior 2021. The Tide class was purchased to support the Queen Elizabeth-class aircraft carriers. (MOD/CROWN COPYRIGHT)

RFA *Tidespring*

The modern day RFA *Tidespring* has taken on the battle honours of the previous RFA *Tidespring,* which served with distinction during the 1982 Falklands Conflict. Her ship's badge was transferred to the new ship and installed during her construction in South Korea.

RFA *Tidespring* took part in the 2021 Carrier Strike Group's ships deployment to the Far East and spent more than seven months on a global mission before returning home. The tanker, along with RFA *Fort Victoria*, kept the task group – nine ships, one submarine, 32 aircraft and more than 3,700 personnel – supplied with everything from fuel to ammunition and food during their 49,000 nautical mile mission.

Tidespring conducted 111 replenishment-at-sea tasks – one every two days while away – supplying fuel and stores to ships from Canada, Denmark, France, India, Italy, Japan, the Netherlands, New Zealand, South Korea, and the United States in addition to the UK.

RFA *TIDESPRING*
Pennant number A136
Ordered: February 2012
Builder: DSME, South Korea
Laid down: December 2014
Launched: April 2015
In service: November 27, 2017
Home port: Marchwood Military Port, Southampton
Status: Active service

RFA *Tiderace*

The second of the Tide class was laid down in December 2014. There was a minor delay to her construction after a fire in the shipyard in South Korea. RFA *Tiderace* eventually sailed from South Korea in June 2017 and headed for the UK via the Panama Canal. When she arrived in Falmouth, Cornwall, the installation of armour, self-defence weaponry and military communications systems took place.

There then followed a period of trials that included deck landings by Royal Navy Merlin HM2 helicopters and replenishment-at-sea trials with the Type 23 frigate, HMS *Somerset*.

Since entering service in August 2018, the ship has taken part in several training exercises in UK waters, including Joint Warrior in spring 2019. In January 2020 she was dry docked at Cammell Laird's shipyard in Birkenhead, Merseyside, for a six-month maintenance period, which included the replacement of her four engine/generator funnel exhausts and an upgrade to her high-pressure saltwater fire main.

RFA *TIDERACE*
Pennant number A137
Ordered: February 2012
Builder: DSME, South Korea
Laid down: June 2015
Launched: November 2015
In service: August 2, 2018
Home port: Marchwood Military Port, Southampton
Status: Active service

a boarding operation to seize the Iranian tanker, *Grace 1*, that had been reported to be heading to Syria in defiance of US sanctions.

RFA *Tideforce*

As the fourth and last ship in the Tide class, RFA *Tideforce* arrived in Falmouth in Cornwall in August 2018 for fitting out with UK-specific equipment. After entering fleet service in July 2019, she took part in replenishment-at-sea exercises with the aircraft carrier HMS *Queen Elizabeth* and the Dutch warship, HNLMS *Friesland*.

In September 2019 the ship RFA *Tideforce* accompanied HMS *Queen Elizabeth* on the three-month Westland 19 deployment to the United States.

After returning home the ship took part in a series of NATO exercises in European waters, supported Royal Navy helicopters in training and participated in a major operation by eight Royal Navy warships to monitor the passage through UK waters of seven Russian warships. In June 2020 she conducted the first-ever night-time replenishment-at-sea of HMS *Queen Elizabeth*.

RFA *TIDEFORCE*
Pennant number A139
Ordered: February 2012
Builder: DSME, South Korea
Laid down: December 24, 2015
Launched: January 21, 2017
In service: July 30, 2019
Home port: Marchwood Military Port, Southampton
Status: Active service

RFA *Tidesurge*

The ship sailed from DSME's shipyard at Okpo in South Korea in November 2017 and began a series of trials with warships of the Republic of Korea Navy. After arriving in the UK the ship was sent to the A&P Group's Falmouth yard in Cornwall for the installation of UK-specific equipment. In November 2018, during her subsequent trials in UK waters, RFA *Tidesurge* became the first Tide-class tanker to receive an RAF Chinook helicopter on her stern landing pad. In February 2019 she conducted her first replenishment-at-sea with the Type 45 destroyer HMS *Defender*. Three months later she carried out the first Tide-to-Tide replenishment-at-sea

when she passed fuel to RFA *Tideforce* during the latter's sea trials.

RFA *Tidesurge* carried a contingent of Royal Marines and Royal Navy Wildcat helicopters to Gibraltar in July 2019, where they launched

RFA *TIDESURGE*
Pennant number A138
Ordered: February 2012
Builder: DSME, South Korea
Laid down: December 7, 2015
Launched: June 4, 2016
In service: February 20, 2019
Home port: Marchwood Military Port, Southampton
Status: Active service

RFA *Argus*

Aviation Training and Medical Support Ship

ABOVE: Fleet Air Arm helicopters pilots use RFA *Argus* to practise ship deck landings. (MOD/CROWN COPYRIGHT)

RFA *ARGUS*	
Builder: Società Italiana Ernesto Breda at Marghera, Venice, Italy	
Launched: November 28, 1980	
Completed: July 31, 1981	
Acquired: March 18, 1988	
Commissioned: June 1, 1988	
Renamed: March 25, 1987	
Home port: HMNB Devonport, Plymouth	
Status: Active service	
Specifications	
Displacement: 28,081 tonnes	
Length: 175.1m (574ft 6in)	
Beam: 30.4m (99ft 9in)	
Draught: 8.1m (26ft 7in)	
Propulsion: 2 × Lindholmen Pielstick 18 PC2.5V diesels	
Speed: 18kts (33kph; 21mph)	
Range: 20,000nm (37,000km; 23,000 miles)	
Complement: 80 RFA, 50 RN, 137 RN air squadron personnel when embarked (200 nursing and medical staff when the hospital is activated)	
Armament	
2 × Oerlikon 20mm/85 KAA on GAM-BO1 mountings, 4 × 7.62mm GPMGs Mk44 Miniguns	
Aviation facilities: 1 aircraft lift from flight deck, 4x hangars	
Aircraft carried: three spots for up to six medium helicopters	

The ship was built as the commercial container ship MV *Contender Bezant* and entered service with the Sea Containers company in 1980. She was part of the fleet of ships taken up from trade to support the Royal Navy during the 1982 Falklands conflict and was converted to carry helicopters to the South Atlantic. After the war she was returned to her owners but in 1984 the Royal Navy decided to buy her to be converted into an aviation training ship.

After being modified at Harland & Wolff in Belfast she formally joined the Royal Fleet Auxiliary in 1988. Three years later she was modified to be a fully functioning field hospital and sailed to support British forces during the first Gulf War.

BELOW: RFA *Argus* has a secondary role as a hospital ship. (MOD/CROWN COPYRIGHT)

Over the next 30 years, RFA *Argus* proved to be highly useful in a variety of roles.

In the 1992 Bosnian crisis she sailed to the Adriatic loaded with 105mm Light Guns and other equipment for a standby force of Royal Marines in case it was necessary to evacuate the British peacekeeping contingent serving with the United Nations.

Then she was mobilised as a hospital ship during the 2003 invasion of Iraq. Five years later she was dispatched to the Indian Ocean as a helicopter platform during the Somalia piracy crisis. In 2014, she was converted back into a hospital ship to join the British-led effort to control the Ebola virus outbreak in Sierra Leone.

Budget pressures led to the Royal Navy looking to retire her in 2024, but delays in building her replacement have meant that she will remain in service until beyond 2030. In July 2022 it was announced that RFA *Argus* would be converted into the first Littoral Strike Ship to carry Royal Marines and combat helicopters.

RFA *Fort Victoria*

At Sea Logistic Support for the Fleet

RFA *Fort Victoria* is the sole surviving vessel of the Fort-class multi-role logistic vessels that were delivered during the 1990s. The ship was designed to carry fuel, food, ammunition, and other supplies to warships using replenishment-at-sea techniques. Stores are moved to deck for transfer by a series of heavy-duty lifts.

She survived a bomb attack in her engine compartment made by the Provisional IRA in 1990, which nearly sunk her during her construction in Belfast. Although prompt action prevented the loss of the vessel, her delivery was delayed by two years.

RFA *Fort Victoria* subsequently gave sterling service to the RFA, including supporting the amphibious landings in southern Iraq in 2003 during Operation Telic. Three years later she supported warships evacuating British nationals from Lebanon during Operation Highbrow.

Her versatility was demonstrated during the Somali piracy crisis when she functioned as a floating base for Royal Marine boarding parties. In 2011 RFA *Fort Victoria* joined US Navy warships to rescue an Italian merchant ship held by pirates. The following year she hosted US Navy helicopters during another anti-piracy patrol off Somalia.

During 2017-2018, she underwent a major refit to allow her to support the new Queen Elizabeth-class aircraft carriers that were in the process of entering service, which included improvements to her fuel tanks to meet new international anti-pollution regulations.

The retirement of her sister ship RFA *Fort George* as a result of the 2010 defence cuts meant RFA *Fort Victoria* was the Royal Navy's only solid support ship capable of transferring bulk ammunition and other supplies to the new Queen Elizabeth-class aircraft carriers. Plans to replace her with new Fleet Solid Support ships have been hit by a serious delay and they will not now be ready until 2028 at the earliest. This delay has dramatically increased the importance of RFA *Fort Victoria* as without her the two carriers' global reach will be severely curtailed. She sailed with the HMS *Queen Elizabeth* during the 2021 Carrier Strike Group to the Far East. However, immediately before sailing she was hit by a fire in Portland Harbour, leading to fears for the viability of the upcoming deployment.

RFA *FORT VICTORIA*		
Pennant number A387		
Ordered: April 23, 1986		
Builder: Harland & Wolff, Belfast Laid down: September 15, 1988		
Launched: May 4, 1990		
Commissioned: June 24, 1994		
Home port: Marchwood Military Port, Southampton		
Status: Active service		
Specifications		
Displacement: 31,565 tons		
Length: 203.5m (667ft 8in)		
Beam: 30.4m (99ft 9in)		
Draught: 9.7m (31ft 10in)		
Propulsion: 2 × Crossley-Pielstick V16 medium speed diesels		
Speed: 20kts (37kph; 23mph)		
Complement: 95 RFA, 15 RN, 24 RNSTS, 154 RN Air Squadron personnel		
Capacity		
12,500 m³ (441,433 cu ft) liquids		
3,377 m³ (119,258 cu ft) ammunition		
2,941 m³ (103,860 cu ft) dry stores		
Armament		
2 × Phalanx CIWS, 2 × GAM-BO1 20mm guns, 3 × Minigun		
7 × General Purpose Machine Guns		
Aviation facilities		
Hangar for 3 × Merlin helicopters		
2-spot flight deck		

LEFT: RFA *Fort Victoria* played a key role in supporting **HMS** *Queen Elizabeth* during the Carrier Strike Group 21 deployment. She is seen here passing through the Suez Canal. (MOD/CROWN COPYRIGHT)

The Point-class Ro-Ro Sea Lift Ships

Moving the British Army around the World

ABOVE: British Army armoured units are routinely deployed around the world on the Point-class ships for exercises and operations.
(MOD/CROWN COPYRIGHT)

Although not officially part of the Royal Fleet Auxiliary, the ships are operated under contract to the Ministry of Defence, in close co-ordination with the Royal Navy. The 1998 Strategic Defence and Security Review identified the need for the UK to have access to large roll-on, roll-off vessels to allow the rapid deployment of large numbers of British Army vehicles and other equipment in time of crisis. During the 1995 Bosnia crisis, the UK had to ask the United States to provide a number of its fast sea lift vessels to move reinforcements to the Balkans.

To reduce costs, the ships were not bought outright for the RFA but purchased under a 22-year Private Finance Initiative, or PFI, contract with their operator, AWSR Shipping Ltd, now known as Foreland Shipping. The company was formed by a consortium of four UK-based shipping companies, Bibby Line, Houlder Hadley Shipping, James Fisher Shipping Services and Andrew Weir Shipping, in 2001. In August 2013 James Fisher plc sold its 25% shareholding in Foreland to the UK-based Hadley Shipping Group, which currently wholly owns Foreland. The six ships were all UK-flagged so they would remain under UK law.

Under the PFI contract the Merchant Navy crews of the ships must be UK citizens and they are all sponsored reservists so they can be mobilised quickly into the Royal Navy. When the ships sail into high-threat regions they are routinely provided with force protection teams of Royal Marines manning machine guns positioned around their decks.

The ships were specifically designed to transport military vehicles and cargos, with enough space to carry all the vehicles required for a British Army armoured battlegroup.

Initially, six ships were built under the contract, two being constructed at Harland & Wolff in Belfast and the

RIGHT: The Point-class ships can dock at most ports with loading facilities and ramps to accommodate large number of vehicles.
(MOD/CROWN COPYRIGHT)

POINT CLASS	
Builders: Flensburger Schiffbau, Germany (4 ships), Harland & Wolff, Belfast (2 ships)	
Operators: Foreland Shipping Ltd (formerly AWSR Ltd)	
In service: 2002–present	
Completed: 6	
Specifications	
Displacement: 23,000 tonnes full load	
Length: 193m (633ft 2in)	
Beam: 26m (85ft 4in)	
Draught: 7.6m (24ft 11in)	
Propulsion: 2 × MaK 94M43 diesel engines	
Speed: 21.5kts (39.8kph; 24.7mph)	
Range: 9,200 nm (17,000km; 10,600 miles)	
Crew: 18–22	
Capacity: 2,650 linear metres of space for vehicles, including	
130 armoured vehicles and 60 trucks and ammunition	
Aviation facilities: Can carry up to four helicopters including Chinook, Apache, Merlin, and Wildcat	

POINT-CLASS SHIPS 2022		
Name	Builder	Commissioned
MV *Hurst Point*	Flensburger Schiffbau	16 August 2002
MV *Hartland Point*	Harland & Wolff, Belfast	11 December 2002
MV *Eddystone*	Flensburger Schiffbau	28 November 2002
MV *Anvil Point*	Harland & Wolff, Belfast	17 January 2003

the Iraq conflict was escalating and they were soon heavily involved in deploying equipment to the Middle East. When the UK involvement in Afghanistan escalated after 2006, the ships were used to ferry vehicles and heavy equipment to ports on Cyprus or in the Middle East, and from there RAF heavy-lift aircraft would then fly the cargo into the land-locked central Asian country.

As a result of the 2010 defence cuts, the Ministry of Defence decided to reduce spending on the ships, so the two that were being held at readiness were dropped from the contract.

In recent years, the Point-class vessels have been heavily involved in moving British Army vehicles and equipment to the Baltic States as part of the build up of NATO forces in the region. The establishment of British Army training centres in Oman and Kenya has also given the ships plenty of work moving cargoes to these new exercise areas.

LEFT: Vehicles are loaded onto Point-class ships via their large rear ramp. (MOD/CROWN COPYRIGHT)

remaining four at the Flensburger Schiffbau shipyard in Germany, to a common design. The first four ships were permanently contracted to the MoD and the other two were at notice for MoD tasking. The two ships – MV *Longstone* and MV *Beachy Head* – could be called into UK service at 20 days' and 30 days' notice respectively. In the meantime, the PFI company chartered them to a civilian ferry operator for service on Baltic routes.

The ships entered service just as the British Army's contribution to

BELOW: More than 100 heavy armoured vehicles can be carried inside Point-class vessels. (MOD/CROWN COPYRIGHT)

Fleet Air Arm in 2022

British Naval Air Power

Britain's Royal Navy has more than a century's experience of flying aircraft from ships and a reputation for innovation. It was one of the first military services to operate airships in 1909 and less than a decade later it commissioned the first ship that could both launch and recover aircraft, HMS *Argus*. The birth of the aircraft carrier era saw the Royal Naval Air Service transition into the Fleet Air Arm of the Royal Air Force. In May 1939 the Fleet Air Arm returned to the control of the Admiralty, just in time for the start of World War Two. In that conflict Royal Navy aviators scored notable successes, sinking the bulk of the Italian fleet at Taranto and then inflicting critical damage to the famous German battleship the *Bismarck*.

The Fleet Air Arm reached its peak in the 1950s and 1960s with the building of angle-deck carriers that embarked jet combat aircraft. The Royal Navy also led the way in embarking helicopters armed with torpedoes and depth charges on warships for anti-submarine missions. Troop-carrying Royal Navy helicopters also conducted the first ship-to-shore assault during the 1956 Suez crisis.

Defence cuts in the 1960s and 1970s clipped the wings of the Fleet Air Arm, but the combination of

the Hawker Siddeley Sea Harriers and the Invincible-class carriers proved instrumental to the successful South Atlantic campaign in 1982 that enabled Britain to recapture the Falkland Islands.

From the 1980s through to 2010 the Royal Navy fielded three Invincible-class carriers, but a brutal round of defence cuts led to the scrapping of these iconic ships and the Hawker Siddeley Harrier GR9s that flew from them. This resulted in a decade in which the Fleet Air Arm only operated helicopters from its warships.

In the past decade the Fleet Air Arm has seen its organisation and structure trimmed back to meet the tight financial circumstances of the era. The old Fleet Air Arm headquarters at Royal Naval Air Station Yeovilton, Somerset, is now just a memory.

Control of British naval aviation is now split between the Assistant Chief of the Naval Staff (Aviation, Amphibious Capability and Carriers) and Rear-Admiral Fleet Air Arm, who controls maritime aviation on warships from Navy Command headquarters in Portsmouth, and the Joint Helicopter Command, which controls the battlefield troop transport helicopters that support the Royal Marine Commando Forces from Headquarters Army in Andover.

The modern Fleet Air Arm is still predominately a rotary wing force, built around variants of the AgustaWestland Merlin and Wildcat platforms.

To dominate sea zones and hunt submarines, the Merlin HM2 operates from carriers, frigates, destroyers, and shore bases. It has a surveillance radar to look for hostile warships and monitors the undersea environment with sonobuoys and dunking sonar. Extensive communications and datalinks allow it to share combat information with warships, aircraft, and shore bases.

Until 2018, 849 NAS operated the old Westland Sea King ASAC7 in the airborne surveillance and control roles, but the unit is preparing to convert to operate the new Crowsnest Airborne Early Warning (AEW) system. This system should be

installed as a roll-on, roll-off kit on standard Merlin MH2 airframes but it has not yet been formally declared fully operational.

The Royal Navy Wildcat Force has the mission to dominate sea zones around naval task groups. Its helicopters have powerful radars and thermal imaging sensors to monitor surface targets, including small patrol boats. In 2021 it began fielding the new Thales Martlet missile that can

be fired in volleys against swarms of enemy patrol boats. The larger MBDA Sea Venom weapon will allow Wildcats to engage bigger warships when it enters service later this decade.

To move Royal Marine assault forces around the battlefield, the Commando Helicopter Force (CHF) is equipped with the Merlin HC3/4. These helicopters are also used for utility tasks within the carrier »

ABOVE: The Fleet Air Arm is now back in the aircraft carrier business with the arrival of HMS *Queen Elizabeth* and HMS *Prince of Wales*, equipped with the F-35B Lightning. (MOD/CROWN COPYRIGHT)

BELOW: Royal Navy personnel are an integral part of the Lightning Force with the RAF's 617 Squadron, operating the F-35B Lightning II. (MOD/CROWN COPYRIGHT)

battlegroup. Some 25 ex-RAF Merlin HC3/3As are now being converted to the HC4/4A configuration under the Merlin Life Sustainment Programme. This incorporates an HM2 standard cockpit as well as folding blades and tail rotors to allow them to be operated from amphibious warfare ships. The first converted HC4/4A was handed over to the CHF in May 2018 and all the helicopters are expected to be converted by 2023.

The Fleet Air Arm is in the process of getting back into the fast jet business after almost a decade since the retirement of the Harrier GR9s, with the Lockheed Martin F-35B Lightning II combat jet now operational from the Royal Navy's two new aircraft carriers, HMS *Queen Elizabeth,* and HMS *Prince of Wales.* 809 Naval Air Squadron »

RIGHT: When employed in the vertical-replenishment role, it is routine for Merlin HC4s to operate from destroyers, frigates, and Royal Fleet Auxiliary ships.
(MOD/CROWN COPYRIGHT)

BELOW: Operating safely from busy aircraft carrier flight decks requires extensive training to ensure Fleet Air Arm personnel are fully qualified for their roles.
(MOD/CROWN COPYRIGHT)

ABOVE: Merlin HM2 anti-submarine helicopters are the core of the air groups embarked on the Queen Elizabeth-class aircraft carriers. (MOD/CROWN COPYRIGHT)

ABOVE: The Crowsnest early warning radar system can be installed on Merlin HM2 helicopters for carrier deployments. (MOD/CROWN COPYRIGHT)

UNIT	AIRCRAFT	BASE	ROLE	NOTES
ROYAL NAVY FLEET AIR ARM SQUADRONS - SEPTEMBER 2022				
Navy Command, Portsmouth				
Flying Squadrons				
809 Naval Air Squadron	F-35B Lightning	RAF Marham	Carrier-borne fighter/strike	To reform in April 2023
814 Naval Air Squadron	Merlin HM2	RNAS Culdrose	Anti-submarine warfare/small ship flight	
815 Naval Air Squadron	Wildcat HMA2	RNAS Yeovilton	Small ship flights	
820 Naval Air Squadron	Merlin HM2	RNAS Culdrose	Anti-submarine warfare/carrier air group	
824 Naval Air Squadron	Merlin HM2	RNAS Culdrose	Conversion Training	
825 Naval Air Squadron	Wildcat HMA2	RNAS Yeovilton	Conversion Training	
700X Naval Air Squadron	Various	RNAS Culdrose	Remotely Piloted Aircraft System- trials unit	
750 Naval Air Squadron	Avenger T1	RNAS Culdrose	Observer grading and training	
FOST Flight	Dauphin	Cornwall Airport, Newquay	Support to Flag Officer Sea Training	
Non-Flying Squadrons				
1700 Naval Air Squadron		RNAS Culdrose	Flight Deck activities, Logistic and Catering Support, Operations, Engineering Support	
1710 Naval Air Squadron		HMNB Portsmouth	Specialist aircraft repair, modifications, and scientific support	
Joint Helicopter Command, Andover				
Commando Helicopter Force, RNAS Yeovilton				
845 Naval Air Squadron	Merlin HC4A/HC4	RNAS Yeovilton	Medium lift	
846 Naval Air Squadron	Merlin HC4A/HC4	RNAS Yeovilton	Medium lift/Merlin HC4 Operational Conversion Unit	
847 Naval Air Squadron	Wildcat AH1	RNAS Yeovilton	Battlefield reconnaissance and support	
Headquarters No 22 Group RAF - Military Flying Training Systems				
703 Naval Air Squadron	Prefect T1	RAF Barkston Heath	Elementary flying training	Part of the Defence Elementary Flying Training School
705 Naval Air Squadron	Juno HT1	RAF Shawbury	Basic and Advanced Single Engine helicopter training	Part of Defence Helicopter Flying School
727 Naval Air Squadron	Tutor T1	RNAS Yeovilton	Pilot grading and Air Experience/ Elementary Flying Training	Part of the Defence Elementary Flying Training School
RAF Air Warfare Centre, RAF Waddington				
744 Naval Air Squadron	Merlin HM2 Crowsnest & Wildcat HMA2	MoD Boscombe Down	Operational Test and Evaluation	Tri-service unit, formerly Mission Systems and Armament Test and Evaluation Squadron RAF

RIGHT: Banshee unmanned aerial vehicles are to be deployed on HMS *Prince of Wales* later this year for her cruise to the United States. (MOD/CROWN COPYRIGHT)

BELOW: 700X Naval Air Squadron is the Royal Navy's experimental unit, currently tasked with trialling a range of unmanned aerial vehicles. (MOD/CROWN COPYRIGHT)

is scheduled to reform in 2023 to become the naval force elements of the Lightning Force. Naval personnel already serve in RAF F-35B squadrons and, when fully formed, all elements of the Lightning Force will contain personnel from both services.

UK naval aviation squadrons are held at varying states of readiness to be mobilised for operations.

The largest Royal Navy aviation deployment of 2021 was the cruise by HMS *Queen Elizabeth* and her carrier strike group to the Far East. This saw a sustained deployment of fast jets on the Royal Navy carrier for the first time in over a decade.

Both HMS *Queen Elizabeth* and HMS *Prince of Wales* are now fully operational and keeping their flight

decks full of aircraft and helicopters is a high priority of the Fleet Air Arm. There are currently only enough F-35B aircraft, pilots, and maintainers to field one air group at a time, so during the remainder of 2022 and into 2023 each carrier will take turns being at high readiness to embark an F-35B air group. While one is so occupied, the other carrier will concentrate on being

a helicopter platform for the Fleet Air Arm, Royal Air Force and Army Air Corps assets.

The NavyX experimental organisation is now tackling several projects aimed at bringing unmanned aerial vehicles (UAVs) into service. These range from small hand-launched drones that can be operated from Royal Marine landing craft, up to large long-endurance systems that can be launched off the deck of the Queen Elizabeth-class carriers by catapult. A possible unmanned replacement for the Crowsnest AEW helicopter is being activity explored.

More than a century from its early experiments operating manned aircraft from the first carriers, the Royal Navy remains at the forefront of developing naval aviation technology.

FLEET AIR ARM INVENTORY, SEPTEMBER 2022	
	Total
Rotary-wing Platforms	
Dauphin	2
Merlin HM2	30
Merlin HC3/3A/4/4A	25
Wildcat HMA2	28
Fixed-wing Platforms	
Avenger T1	4
F-35B Lightning (shared with RAF)	26

Source: UK Armed Forces Equipment and Formations annual report by UK Ministry of Defence

ABOVE: The Wildcat HMA2 maritime helicopter is the Royal Navy's primary small ships helicopter in armed attack, surveillance, and utility roles. (MOD/CROWN COPYRIGHT)

BELOW: Merlin HC4/3A assault helicopter crews of the Commando Helicopter Force are trained to operate in a range of operational environments, including inside the Arctic Circle. (MOD/CROWN COPYRIGHT)

F-35B Lightning

Carrier Strike Jet

ABOVE: The F-35B Lightning is the only in-production vertical take-off and landing combat aircraft in the world. (MOD/CROWN COPYRIGHT)

The F-35B Lightning is the vertical take-off and landing (VTOL) variant of the international Joint Strike Fighter (JSF). It is fitted with a revolutionary lift fan and rotating jet nozzle to control the final stages of landing and take-off.

The United States Marine Corps (USMC) and the UK were the prime drivers of the variant, with the intention of building a replacement for the stalwart AV-8B Harrier family of jump jets. Under existing plans, the USMC intends to purchase 353 aircraft and the UK plans to have 48 on contract to equip the air wings of the two Queen Elizabeth-class carriers by 2025. A second tranche of 26 F-35Bs has been approved for delivery by the end of the decade.

For operators, the F-35B will bring both the VTOL capabilities of the old Harrier as well as the stealth, or low observable, capabilities of fifth-generation combat aircraft. When flying in full-on stealth mode, all weapons are carried in the internal weapons bay. For missions that do not require stealth flight profiles the aircraft has several wing pylons that carry additional weapons.

The lift fan and rotating nozzle have vastly different properties to the Harrier's four rotating jet nozzles, so aircraft carrier decks and runways have to be protected with special heat-resistant coatings.

The Royal Navy shares ownership of the UK's F-35Bs with the Royal Air Force, via the Lightning Force at RAF Marham in Norfolk. It currently has two flying units, 617 and 207 Squadrons of the RAF, with the latter unit being the operational conversion one. RAF and Royal Navy personnel serve in both units. The Royal Navy-badged F-35 unit, 809 Naval Air Squadron, is expected to stand up during 2023. UK F-35Bs have also flown operational missions over Iraq and Syria but have not released live ordnance. One was lost in an accident in 2021.

RIGHT: HMS *Queen Elizabeth*'s air group has been built around the F-35B Lightning. (MOD/CROWN COPYRIGHT)

Wildcat: Armed Helicopter

Strike Power for the Royal Navy and Royal Marines

The Royal Navy operates both land-based and maritime variants of the AgustaWestland Wildcat helicopter, which was an evolution of the famous Westland Lynx.

Two LHTEC CTS800 turboshaft engines power both variants of the Wildcat and they also share a common nose-mounted thermal-imaging sensor. The main difference is that the Royal Navy Wildcat HMA2 were fitted with the Sea Spray radar as standard to allow them to monitor naval targets, whilst the Wildcat AH1s operated by the Army Air Corps (AAC) and 847 Naval Air Squadron (NAS) were not fitted with the radar as a cost-saving measure.

A prototype Wildcat first flew in 2009 and the first land variant entered service with the Army Air Corps in 2014. The Royal Navy started operating its first HMA2 in 2015. All the Royal Navy and Fleet Air Arm Wildcats are based together at RNAS Yeovilton in Somerset to allow savings to be made in training, operating and maintenance costs.

The Royal Navy Wildcat Force is based around two flying squadrons. 815 NAS provides flights of one or two of the 28 Wildcat HMA2 maritime variants to be embarked on Royal Navy frigates and destroyers. Meanwhile, Wildcat crews are trained by instructors from 825 NAS to fly the helicopters. The core work of the Wildcat HMA2 is to provide single

helicopters to operate from frigates and destroyers. Since the entry to service of the Queen Elizabeth-class aircraft carriers, Wildcat detachments have also operated from their decks in a force-protection role.

The third unit of the CHF is 847 NAS, which flies the land variant of the Wildcat, the AH1. The CHF and AAC Wildcat units share a common pool of 34 air frames.

In 2021 the Wildcat HMA2 was cleared to operate the Thales Martlet anti-ship missile, using a special launcher that allows a helicopter to carry 20 missiles for use against swarms of small patrol boats. Work is underway to install MBDA Sea Venom heavy anti-ship missiles to allow the helicopters to engage large enemy vessels.

WILDCAT HMA2		
In service: 2015 onwards		
Used by: Royal Navy		
Manufacturer: AgustaWestland/Leonardo		
Produced: 2009 to 2015		
Number built: 28		
Crew: 2 pilots		
Capacity: 6 passengers, including door gunner		
Length: 15.24m (50ft)		
Height: 3.73m (12ft 3in)		
Max take-off weight: 6,000kg (13,228lb)		
Powerplant: 2 × LHTEC CTS800-4N turboshaft		
Maximum speed: 311kph (193mph, 168 kts)		
Range: 420nm (777km; 483 miles)		
Endurance: 2hr 15min (4hr 30min with auxiliary fuel tanks)		
Armament		
Pintle-mounted machine gun, e.g., FN MAG (Army) or Browning M3M (Navy)		
Air-to-surface missile systems		
Up to 20x Thales Martlet (Lightweight Multirole Missile), formerly Future Anti-Surface Guided Weapon (Light)		
Up to 4×MBDA Sea Venom, formerly Future Anti-Surface Guided Weapon (Heavy),		
Sting Ray torpedo and Mk 11 depth charges		

ABOVE: As well as being heavily armed with Martlet and Sea Venom missiles, Royal Navy Wildcat HMA2s are versatile utility helicopters. (MOD/CROWN COPYRIGHT)

BELOW: The Wildcat HMA2 is the Royal Navy's primary helicopter embarked on frigates and destroyers. (MOD/CROWN COPYRIGHT)

Merlin:
Work Horse of the Fleet

Multi-Role Helicopter

ABOVE: The Merlin is the workhorse of the fleet.
(MOD/CROWN COPYRIGHT)

RIGHT: Anti-submarine and anti-surface operations are conducted by the Merlin HM2, which has specialist sensors to detect targets above and below the water.
(MOD/CROWN COPYRIGHT)

Work on the helicopters that eventually became the AgustaWestland AW101 Merlin formally got underway in 1981. It was intended to replace the Royal Navy's anti-submarine and troop-carrying Westland Sea Kings.

The three-engine Merlin was designed as part of a joint British-Italian project, with assembly of the Royal Navy's helicopters taking place the Yeovil plant of Westland Helicopters, then AgustaWestland and now Leonardo.

The first anti-submarine variant, the Merlin HM1 entered service with the Royal Navy in 1999. The first 44 helicopters were fitted with the Blue Kestrel surface surveillance radar, a dipping sonar and launchers for sonobuoys, and they were also equipped with the Stingray torpedo. Lockheed Martin was responsible for integrating the helicopter's weapons system. In 2006 the US company was contracted to upgrade 30 of the Merlins to new HM2 standard. These

helicopters featured new cockpit avionics and a new mission system. The first of the modified helicopters entered service in 2014. The Merlin HM2 helicopters are all based at RNAS Culdrose in Cornwall when not embarked on Royal Navy warships.

Dedicated support to the Royal Marines of 3 Commando Brigade is provided by a specialist unit, Commando Helicopter Force (CHF), based at Yeovilton, Somerset, which operates Merlin troop-carrying helicopters.

MERLIN HM2	
In service: 2014 onwards	
Used by: Royal Navy	
Manufacturer: Lockheed Martin (prime contractor), AgustaWestland/Leonardo (platform)	
Produced: 2005 to 2014	
Number built: 30 converted from Merlin HM1	
Specifications	
Powerplant: 3 × Rolls-Royce Turbomeca RTM322-01 turboshaft engines	
Max take-off weight: 14,600kg (32,187lb)	
Cruise speed: 150kts (278 kph; 173mph)	
Range: 450nm (833km; 518 miles)	
Endurance: 5 hours	
Crew: 3–4	
Capacity:	
26 troops (38 passengers), 5 tonnes of payload or 4 stretchers (with sonar array removed)	
Avionics	
Selex Galileo Blue Kestrel 5000 maritime surveillance radar	
Active/passive sonobuoys	
Thales 2189 dipping sonar array	
Armament	
Bombs: 4× Sting Ray homing torpedoes or Mk 11 depth charges	
Door Guns: 1 x .50cal machine gun	

ABOVE: Merlin HC4s of the Commando Helicopter Force are often found north of the Arctic Circle supporting the Royal Marines. (MOD/CROWN COPYRIGHT)

It is provided with its own mobile command centre, logistic support and cargo-handling facilities to allow it to operate from Royal Navy amphibious warships or ashore in combat zones. The CHF reports to the tri-service Joint Helicopter Command, which controls all the UK's battlefield helicopters. Its main units are 845 and 846 Naval Air Squadrons, which can trace their heritage in the commando role back to the 1960s. They are still affectionately known as 'Jungles' from their days operating in the Malaysian jungles. The CHF was for a long time associated with the Sea King HC4, but 845 and 846 Naval Air Squadrons now fly the troop-carrying variant of the AgustaWestland Merlin. Starting in 2014, these helicopters were transferred from the RAF. Under the Merlin Life Sustainment Programme, the 25 ex-RAF Merlin HC3/3As are now being converted to the HC4/4A configuration, which includes a folding tail.

The Royal Navy's AgustaWestland Merlin HM2 Crowsnest airborne surveillance and control (ASaC) helicopters formally entered service with 820 Naval Air Squadron in March 2021, ahead of their deployment on HMS *Queen Elizabeth* for the Carrier Strike Group 21 cruise to the Far East.

The distinctive-looking helicopter has a large radar dome or 'bag' that

sticks out from its fuselage, earning it the affectionate nickname of 'bagger'. This was first used by the old airborne early warning Sea Kings, which flew with 849 Naval Air Squadron until 2018.

The ASaC Merlin's new mission systems and Searchwater 2000 radars are provided by Thales UK and installed by aerospace company Leonardo in Yeovil, Somerset, overseen by prime contractor Lockheed Martin. Ten sets of Crowsnest equipment have been purchased. They are designed to be rapidly installed on Merlin helicopters according to operational requirements.

The Crowsnest project has been plagued by technical problems, though, and it missed its 2019 target to enter service. The three Crowsnest Merlins that took part in the Carrier Strike Group 21 deployment were all

pre-Initial Operational Capability (IOC) equipment sets that were not fully certified. Full IOC was scheduled for September 2021, but the Ministry of Defence has not formally declared the system to have met this milestone. Full Operational Capability is now scheduled for May 2023.

BELOW: The Crowsnest airborne early warning helicopter is the latest Merlin variant to enter Royal Navy's service. (MOD/CROWN COPYRIGHT)

History of the Royal Marines

Britain's Amphibious Warriors

RIGHT: Yomping to victory. Royal Marines march into Port Stanley in the Falkland Islands on the day of the Argentine surrender in June 1982.
(MOD/CROWN COPYRIGHT)

RIGHT: Colonel Robert Laycock led one of the first Commando units during World War Two. His aggressive and unconventional methods were well suited to the raiding operations of the early Commandos. (IWM)

British naval captains have long employed heavily armed men on their ships to enforce discipline and function as landing parties on hostile coastlines. Sir Francis Drake sometimes used infantry soldiers aboard his fleet as snipers in the riggings. But it was not until 1672 that the term 'marine' was officially used to denote the new maritime infantry.

The first official unit of marines was initially known as the Duke of Albany's Maritime Regiment and became the Admiral's Regiment on October 28, 1664, which is officially recognised as the founding day of the Corps of Royal Marines. Later these men became known as marines and in 1802 they were given the official title of Royal Marines by King George III.

These early marines won their famous battle honours by helping to capture Gibraltar from Spain in 1704. Marine units played an important part in the American War of Independence and the establishing of the first British colonies in Australia. During the Imperial campaigns of the Victorian era they become the Royal Marine Light Infantry.

In World War One, the Royal Marines played an important role in setting up the Royal Naval Division, which led the campaign to protect the Belgium port of Antwerp. They then took part in the ill-fated Gallipoli landings that failed to secure the Dardanelles Strait near the Turkish capital, Istanbul. In the first major commando raid of the 20th century, Royal Marines took part in the 1918 assault on the German controlled port of Zeebrugge in Belgium.

After British troops were driven from mainland Europe in 1940, the Royal Marines found themselves in the forefront of taking the fight back to Nazi-controlled territories. The Royal Marine Division become the first large formation of troops trained in conducting amphibious landings

and many of its personnel became the first crews of newly introduced landing craft.

These first Commandos were originally part of the British Army, established in 1941 on the orders of Winston Churchill. From their achievements in the early years, the demand for specialist troops grew rapidly. In 1942 units of Royal Marine infantry began converting to the new Commando role. They subsequently took part in the Dieppe and D-Day Landings. Other Royal Marines were trained to conduct sabotage operations using small canoes, or kayaks, under the cover name of the Royal Marines Boom Patrol Detachment (RMBPD). These evolved into the Special Boat Section that carried out naval raids around the Mediterranean.

At the end of World War Two the British Army disbanded its Commandos units but the

Royal Marines decided to adopt the traditions of this elite force permanently. The Royal Marines created a standing formation – 3

Commando Brigade – that was organised, equipped, and trained for amphibious operations. No longer would the Royal Navy have to reinvent its amphibious capability in a time of crisis, it would become a core competency of the British Naval Service. Projecting land power ashore would be the job of the Royal Marines. The Royal Navy supported the Royal Marines by building and operating specialist amphibious shipping that was capable of launching landing craft to carry troops, vehicles, and stores ashore.

The Royal Marines led the way in developing new amphibious warfare tactics, techniques, and equipment. In 1956, during the brief Suez campaign, they conducted the first-ever assault using helicopters to land troops ashore. After providing an amphibious rapid reaction force in the Far East and Middle East during the 1960s, 3 Commando Brigade was re-roled in the early 1970s to support NATO's northern flank in Norway.

3 Commando Brigade played a leading role in the 1982 Falklands Conflict and this dramatically demonstrated the value of retaining a robust amphibious capability. The Royal Marines carried out a major amphibious assault to capture the al-Faw peninsula in the opening hours of the 2003 invasion of Iraq. Units of 3 Command Brigade were also employed in a land role in Afghanistan between 2002 and 2011.

The 2010 Defence Review reduced the readiness level of 3 Commando Brigade so that only one battalion-sized commando unit was held on alert or at high readiness to conduct amphibious operations at short notice. As a result, the size of the amphibious shipping fleet has been reduced, saving considerable sums of money.

Royal Marine Fighting Units

3 Commando Brigade in 2022

RIGHT: Amphibious landing exercises are at the heart of the Royal Marines' training cycle. (MOD/CROWN COPYRIGHT)

As a result of the Future Commando Force initiative that got underway in 2017, the Royal Marines began to restructure 3 Commando Brigade away from predominately manoeuvre, conventional-combat operations to smaller-scale missions in littoral environments.

The reorganisation of the Corps will see the evolution of 3 Commando Brigade into a maritime special operations formation with small contingents, deployed in the Mediterranean and, potentially, the Pacific aboard two littoral strike ships (LSS). Final approval for these LSS has yet to be announced but it would appear that two serving support vessels will be refitted to carry a company group of marines, two Chinooks and two Apache AH64E helicopters.

The move away from battalion-sized operations coincided with the entry to service of the two Queen Elizabeth-class aircraft carriers,

BELOW: It is the job of 47 Commando Raiding Group to land Royal Marines on hostile shores in raiding boats and landing craft. (MOD/CROWN COPYRIGHT)

which have an air assault capability but not an amphibious role. The Royal Marines were mandated to provide embarked contingents on the two carriers whenever they sailed, able to conduct combat search-and-rescue missions to recover downed aircrew.

The old structure of three battalion-sized Commando units trained and equipped solely for amphibious operations also had to be adapted considerably. Each of the main Commando units was given a specialist mission within the Future Commando Force structure.

40 Commando became the dedicated experimental and trials unit, with a remit to evaluate new equipment, tactics, and techniques. The ultimate aim of these experimental efforts is to enable small groups of a few dozen Royal Marines to have the same combat effectiveness as old company-sized contingents of over 100 troops. For example, employing swarms of

mini drones could allow a couple of Royal Marines to monitor dozens of square kilometres of ground without hundreds of soldiers having to physically occupy it.

42 Commando took on the maritime security role, with its personnel providing small boarding and raiding detachments on board Royal Navy warships. As mandated by the Future Commando Force initiative the unit provides embarked contingents on the two carriers able to conduct combat search-and-rescue missions, known as Joint Personnel Recovery (JPR). It also provides maritime security teams to protect Royal Fleet Auxiliary support ships or Point-class roll-on, roll off ships sailing in high-threat regions.

45 Commando retained the conventional war fighting and amphibious role, but with a focus on the High North of Norway and the Arctic region.

The Royal Marines' landing craft and small boats are now grouped under 47 Commando Raiding Group and they provide detachments to serve on amphibious ships or from shore bases.

30 Commando is the brigade's specialist reconnaissance, signals intelligence and information analysis unit. It contains the Special Reconnaissance Squadron which is trained and equipped to make covert landings on hostile coasts by submarine or air.

The Commando Logistic Regiment has the job of providing administrative, medical, logistic, motor transport and other support elements to deployed units of the brigade.

One unique unit within 3 Commando Brigade is 43 Commando which is the modern-day successor to the old Comacchio Company that was formed in the 1970s to protect North Sea oil rigs from terrorist attacks. It is now dedicated to protecting the UK nuclear deterrent both at its base at Faslane and on the road convoys that move nuclear warheads to the Atomic Weapons Establishment at Aldermaston, Berkshire. It is highly trained in maritime security operations to protect the Royal Navy's nuclear submarines as they arrive or depart from Faslane and to launch counterstrikes to retake any facilities linked to the UK nuclear deterrent that might be captured by terrorists or other hostile forces.

The final element of 3 Commando Brigade is its supporting British Army units, trained to support amphibious operations.

The Commando Gunners of 29 Regiment provide gun batteries with the 105mm Light Gun that can be flown ashore by helicopter or moved by landing craft. They also provide forward artillery and air control teams to operate with Commando units. These teams are experts at calling down fire support from 105mm Light Guns as well as naval gunfire support from warships and air strikes by fast jets or helicopter gunships.

3 COMMANDO BRIGADE ORDER OF BATTLE, SEPTEMBER 2022		
ROYAL MARINES UNITS	BRITISH ARMY UNITS	ROYAL NAVY UNITS
30 Commando Information Exploitation Group, Plymouth	24 Commando Regiment, Royal Engineers, Chivenor	Commando Helicopter Force
40 Commando, Taunton	29 Commando Regiment, Royal Artillery, Plymouth	845 Naval Air Squadron
42 Commando, Bickleigh	383 Commando Petroleum Troop (V), Plymouth (att'd Cdo Log Reg)	846 Naval Air Squadron
43 Commando Fleet Protection Group, Faslane	Commando Troop, 821 (EOD & Search) Squadron, 33 Engineer Regiment (EOD&S)	847 Naval Air Squadron
45 Commando, Arbroath		
47 Commando Raiding Group, Plymouth		
Commando Logistic Regiment, Chivenor		
539 Raiding Squadron, Plymouth		

LEFT: Royal Marines of 40 Commando during an Arctic survival exercise in Norway with TV celebrity Bear Grylls (fourth from left), who is an honorary colonel in the Royal Marines Reserve. (MOD/CROWN COPYRIGHT)

LEFT: The Commando Logistic Regiment provides 30 Commando Brigade with its road transport and other support capability. It also has heavily armed Jackal patrol vehicles to protect its road convoys from enemy ambushes. (MOD/CROWN COPYRIGHT)

BELOW: Offshore Raiding Craft and other landing vessels have an important role in the new Future Commando Force concept in operating covertly in disputed coastal regions. (MOD/CROWN COPYRIGHT)

Royal Marines' Weapons and Equipment

Arming the Commandos

The Royal Marines are equipped with specialist weapons and equipment for their unique role as Britain's dedicated amphibious force.

ABOVE: In June 2020 the Royal Marines introduced its new uniform with its distinctive multi-camouflage pattern made by the US company Crye Precision. Royal Marines personnel in specialist roles are also receiving the US-designed Colt AR-15 assault rifle. (MOD/CROWN COPYRIGHT)

ABOVE: The L85A2 assault rifle is the latest version of the SA-80 still used by the Royal Marines. (MOD/CROWN COPYRIGHT)

LEFT: Heavily armed Offshore Raiding Craft (ORC) are used to deliver Royal Marines to enemy held coastlines. The vessels are operated by 47 Commando (Raiding Group) Royal Marines, which was formally titled 1 Assault Group. ORC's can carry 12 Royal Marines and have a forward gun mount for a General Purpose Machine Gun (GPMG) or 40mm grenade launcher. (MOD/CROWN COPYRIGHT)

ABOVE LEFT: Cross-country mobility is provided by the Swedish-made Viking amphibious armoured vehicles. The 99 still in service are operated by the Royal Marines Armoured Support Group. (MOD/CROWN COPYRIGHT)

ABOVE RIGHT: 40 Commando Royal Marines have been experimenting with a range of commercially available so-called hobby drones, to assess out new tactics and procedures for using unmanned aerial vehicles in a variety of scenarios. (MOD/CROWN COPYRIGHT)

LEFT: Royal Marines are put ashore on the beach by the Landing Craft Vehicle Personnel (LCVP) Mark 5. It is 15.5m long by 4.3m wide and capable of carrying 35 fully equipped Royal Marines or vehicles such as the Viking. (MOD/CROWN COPYRIGHT)

LEFT: Large armoured vehicles, including British Army Challenger 2 main battle tanks can be carried in the Landing Craft Utility Mark 10. The 47 Commando (Raiding Group) Royal Marines operates 10 of these highly versatile craft. (MOD/CROWN COPYRIGHT)

Training Tomorrow's Commandos

The Making of Royal Marines

ABOVE LEFT: The Commando Memorial at Spean Bridge.
(PHIL SANGWELL)

ABOVE RIGHT: All budding Royal Marines have to have a good head for heights to pass the Commando Training Course.
(MOD/CROWN COPYRIGHT)

Just to the north of Fort William on the west coast of Scotland is one of Britain's most impressive war memorials. Looking out over the spectacular Lochaber countryside are three World War Two Commandos. Just underneath their feet is the inscription "United we conquer". At the foot of the memorial is a plaque saying: "In memory of the officers and men of the Commandos who died in the Second World War 1939–1945. This country was their training ground."

Situated around a mile from Spean Bridge, the Commando Memorial overlooks the training areas of the Commando Training Depot established in 1942 at nearby Achnacarry Castle.

The exploits of these first British Commandos are legendary and the modern-day Royal Marines have tried to maintain the spirit and ethos of the World War Two warriors in their current Commando Training Course. To win the right to wear the famous Green Beret every Royal Marine must pass the 32-week course at the Commando Training Centre at Lympstone in Devon. Colleagues from the British Army serving in 3 Commando Brigade have their own shorter course, known as the All Arms Commando Course.

The culmination of the Commando Training course is a final exercise and the four Commando tests. The first part of the exercise is the endurance test, where potential Royal Marines have 73 minutes (71 minutes for officers) to work their way through two miles of tunnels, pools, streams, bogs, and woods, then run four miles back to camp and achieve a six out of ten in a shooting test.

Then comes the nine-mile speed march, which has to be completed in 90 minutes while carrying full fighting equipment and a rifle. Next is the famous Tarzan aerial assault course that has to be completed in 13 minutes (12 minutes for officers), also carrying fighting equipment and rifle. The finale is the 30-mile march across Dartmoor, which has to be completed in fewer than eight hours or seven hours for officers, again carrying fighting equipment and a rifle.

Successful Royal Marines then progress to specialist role training before being assigned to a unit within 3 Commando Brigade.

RIGHT: The coveted Green Beret is the ultimate prize for those who successfully pass Royal Marines selection.
(MOD/CROWN COPYRIGHT)

Special Boat Service

Britain's Maritime Strike Force

Britain's elite maritime Special Forces unit is the Special Boat Service (SBS) of the Royal Marines. It traces its history back to World War Two when it was formed as a raiding unit, known as the Special Boat Section, operating in small kayaks launched from submarines or warships. Its motto is 'By Strength and Guile'.

In 1973 the unit was renamed Special Boat Squadron and it went on to play a prominent role in the 1982 Falklands conflict. The SBS was re-organised and expanded in 1987 when the new tri-service Special Forces Group was set up to bring together the British Army's Special Air Service Regiment and the Royal Air Force special forces units. This resulted in the Special Boat Squadron being renamed the Special Boat Service, which took over the global maritime counterterrorist mission from its base at Poole in Dorset.

Covert insertion by sea is the raison d'être of the SBS and its personnel are trained and equipped to approach their targets in small boats or underwater using diver-delivery vehicles. SBS operatives are also trained to parachute into the sea with all their equipment, which allows them to strike at targets around the world at very short notice. In the counterterrorist role, SBS personnel are trained and equipped to approach and board ships and offshore oil platforms of all shapes and sizes. To get aboard fast-moving ships the SBS has high-speed Rigid Inflatable Boats (RIBs). SBS troopers are also trained to fast-rope down onto ships from helicopters.

The SBS and Fleet Air Arm provide troops and helicopters on 24/7 alert, ready to respond to maritime terrorist or hijacking incidents in British territorial waters.

ABOVE: The Special Boat Service is the Royal Marines' elite special forces unit. (MOD/CROWN COPYRIGHT)

BELOW: Mounting covert insertion operations from Royal Navy nuclear submarines is a key skill for the Special Boat Service. (MOD/CROWN COPYRIGHT)

Russian and Chinese Naval Threats in the 21st Century

Today's Threats, Tomorrow's Challenges

"While we see Russia as the clear and present danger, China is posing the long-term challenge."

Admiral Sir Ben Key, First Sea Lord, July 2022

ABOVE: **RFS** *Severodvinsk* is one of the new generation of ultra-quiet Russian nuclear-powered attack boats. She is seen here being shadowed by **HMS** *Portland*. (MOD/CROWN COPYRIGHT)

RIGHT: The introduction of the *Dreadnought* battleship by the Royal Navy in 1905 sparked an arms race as every navy wanted to have these powerful ships. A similar naval arms race is underway today. (JACOBST)

A round the globe the Royal Navy is facing an array of threats and challenges from Russia, China, and several other potentially hostile navies. These involve not just efforts to build new warships, submarines and naval aviation, but a concerted drive by Moscow and Beijing to develop new and innovative weapons that threaten the capabilities of Britain's own warships and weapons systems.

This 21st century naval arms race harks back to the decades before World War One when global navies were locked in a struggle to put bigger and more powerful battleships into service. When the Royal Navy began building the first HMS *Dreadnought* in 1905 it rendered every other battleship obsolete. Within months every major navy was rushing to build rival ships that could meet the Royal Navy on equal terms.

In European waters the main threat to the Royal Navy comes from Russia's fleets that are based off the Barents Sea near Murmansk, in the Baltic and in the Black Sea. While Russia's

RFS *BELGOROD*
Oscar II-class submarine/unmanned underwater vehicle submarine mother ship
Pennant Number K-329
Builder: Sevmash
Laid down: 24 July, 1992
Launched: 23 April, 2019
Commissioned: 8 July, 2022
Specifications
Displacement: 24,000/30,000 tonnes submerged
Length: 184m (603ft 8in)
Beam: 15m (49ft 3in)
Propulsion: Two pressurised water reactor OK-650M.02 nuclear reactors, two shafts
Speed: 32kts (59kph; 37mph) surfaced
Range: Unlimited
Endurance: 120 days
Complement: 110 sub-mariners
Armament: 6 Poseidon drones
Status: In service

ABOVE: **Russian warships moving through the Dover Strait are closely monitored by the Royal Navy.** (MOD/CROWN COPYRIGHT)

3M22 ZIRCON
Type: Hypersonic cruise missile
In service: 2022
Used by: Russian Navy
Designer: NPO Mashinostroyeniya
Manufacturer: NPO Mashinostroyeniya
Produced: 2021–present
Specifications
Length: 9m (30ft)
Diameter: 60cm (24in)
Maximum firing range: 1,500km (930 miles)
Warhead: > 300 HE, >200 kt tnw nuclear
Warhead weight: 300–400kg (660–880lb)
Engine: Scramjet
Operational range: >540nm (1,000km; 620 miles)
Maximum speed: Mach 5 – Mach 9 (6,100–11,000kph; 1.7–3.1 kps; 3,800–6,900mph)
Launch platform: Submarine, surface ship, land-based (in development)

aircraft carrier, cruisers, destroyers, and frigates are not a match for their counterparts in British and NATO service, the country's submarines and missiles pose a major threat.

Russia's submarine force may be a shadow of the massive Soviet submarine threat, but the Kremlin has continued to invest in new underwater technology and its current generation of submarines is believed to be quiet – hence harder to detect – and boasts an armoury of modern weapons, including Kalibr precision-guided land-attack cruise missiles.

New attack and ballistic missile-carrying submarines are under construction, so a constant drum beat of new boats is set to be delivered over the coming decade. The Russian Navy is also investing heavily in a new family of multi-role submarines that can launch mini-submarines or unmanned underwater vehicles on covert missions against enemy coastal infrastructure or underwater structures. Royal Navy

chiefs have expressed fears that this development poses a serious threat to the UK and international communications cables that run under the North Atlantic, carrying a major chunk of the world's internet communications. The first of these 'mother ship' submarines, the RFS *Belgorod,* formally entered service with the Russian Northern Fleet in July 2022. This vessel is also expected to carry the new Poseidon unmanned underwater vehicle, which is reported to have an oceanic range and the capacity to be fitted with thermonuclear warheads to devastate hostile naval bases.

Russia is also rolling out a new generation of hypersonic missiles that could potentially transform naval warfare. Its first hypersonic weapon, the Zircon, is already in service on Russian Admiral Gorshkov-class frigates. The weapon has a speed in excess of Mach 5, which would allow it to defeat enemy air defences before they have time to react. Versions of »

BELOW: **A Russian Naval Aviation Su-30SMs buzzed HMS *Defender* repeatedly when she entered Russian-controlled waters around the disputed Crimea peninsular.** (MOD/CROWN COPYRIGHT)

ABOVE: Chinese J-15 fighter jets now operate from the PLAN's aircraft carriers and pose a serious threat to naval forces in the Pacific region. (PLAN)

BELOW: The J-31 is China's first stealth fighter and its deployment is part of a concerted drive by the Chinese military to challenge US air supremacy. (PLAN)

RFS *ADMIRAL KUZNETSOV*
Kuznetsov-class aircraft carrier
Pennant number 063
Ordered: March 3, 1981
Builder: Nikolayev South
Designer: Nevskoye Planning and Design Bureau
Laid down: April 1, 1982
Launched: December 6, 1985
Commissioned: January 20, 1991; fully operational in 1995
Status: Undergoing refit
Specifications
Displacement: 57,700 long tons
Length: 305m (1,001ft)
Beam: 72m (236ft)
Draft: 10m (33ft)
Propulsion: Eight turbo-pressurised boilers and four fixed-pitch propellers
Speed: 29kts (54kph; 33mph)
Complement: 1,690 ship's crew and 626 air group personnel
Armament: six AK-630 300m anti-aircraft guns, eight CADS-N-1 Kashtan CIWS and the 3K87 Kortik surface-to-air missile system, 12 P-700 Granit surface-to-surface missiles and the 3K95 Kinzhal surface-to-air missile system, RBU-12000 UDAV-1 ASW rocket launchers
Aircraft carried: 30 aircraft and helicopters

the missile are to be fitted to Russian submarines and installed in shore-based anti-ship missile batteries. This combination of weapons is part of Russia's anti-access, area denial (A2AD) concept which aims at keeping Western warships far from the country's coastlines. This strategy has been employed in the Black Sea in Russia's war with Ukraine and aims to keep Kiev's fleet trapped in port and deter intervention by NATO naval forces.

In the Pacific region, the Chinese Navy offers a very different threat in terms of scale and technology. Last year China spent $293bn on defence, growing its defence budget for the 27th consecutive year. Its expenditure is more than four times that of Russia.

Beijing's naval forces are on a very different scale to those of Russia and dwarf the size of other navies in the

Pacific region. The Chinese surface fleet is enormous, with 51 destroyers, 49 frigates, 70 corvettes and 109 missile boats. These are backed by 79 submarines, including at least six nuclear-powered attack boats and one ballistic missile-firing boat.

The Chinese amphibious landing force has 40,000 marines, who can be embarked on four helicopter carriers and eight amphibious dock ships, as well as more than 60 smaller landing ships.

To boost the striking power of its surface vessels and submarines, the People's Liberation Army Navy (PLAN) has invested heavily in aviation, both shore-based and carrier-borne. It currently has two operational aircraft carriers, with two more under construction. Chinese naval aviation has more than 700

aircraft and helicopters. Although a sizeable chunk of them are old Cold War-era machines, there are plenty of modern aircraft, including fourth generation fighters.

In June this year, the PLAN launched its third aircraft carrier, the

Fujian. This is the first Chinese carrier to rival the US Nimitz-class in size and the first to shift from a ski ramp to electromagnetic catapults to launch fighter aircraft. It is expected to be capable of carrying an air group of 40 jet fighters, backed by embarked airborne early warning aircraft. This will turn China's navy into a true, blue water aircraft carrier force and allow it to project power far from its coastal waters.

The final component in the growth of Chinese naval power has been the build-up of its coastal defence missile forces. These provide a layered defence, and the latest YJ-18 weapon can hit targets up to 500 kilometres from shore.

China's naval strategy is an evolution of Russia's A2AD concept, aimed at making it very difficult for the US and other Western navies to operate close to its coast. At the same time, China's growing blue water navy gives it the capability to challenge the US and its allies in their home waters.

The summer of 2022 saw the Chinese put on a show of naval power around the disputed island of Taiwan, with missile tests and air exercises taking place around its coasts. This appeared to be a rehearsal for an expanded Chinese operation to blockade Taiwan and prevent the US Navy from intervening to stop an amphibious landing.

Both Russia and China have also invested heavily in space-based surveillance satellites to monitor naval moves in real-time. These satellites monitor the heat signature of ships or use radar to track them. This gives Moscow and Beijing the ability to track all naval movement around their coasts and far out to sea. Achieving

surprise in the 21st century is very difficult.

The current generation of Russian naval commanders and sailors can draw on the experience of several generations of their Soviet predecessors, including sustained use of nuclear-powered submarines and carrier operations. For the Chinese, the situation is very different and their naval personnel – of all ranks – are having to learn on the job how to operate ballistic missile-firing submarines and how to catapult aircraft off carriers. This lack of experience will be a problem for the Chinese for many years to come and will give Western navies, including the Royal Navy, an edge in any confrontation with Beijing's navy in the near future.

How long that advantage lasts is the $64,000 question for modern naval strategists.

PLAN'S *FUJIAN*	
Class and type:	Type 003 aircraft carrier
Builder:	Jiangnan Shipyard
Laid down:	March 2015 - February 2016
Launched:	17 June, 2022
Status:	Fitting out
General characteristics	
Displacement:	>80,000 tonnes (79,000 long tons [full load]
Length:	316m (1,036ft 9in) (o/a)
Beam:	76m (249ft 4in) (o/a)
Propulsion:	Steam turbines, 8 boilers, 4 shafts
Aviation facilities:	Hangar deck

ABOVE: The Chinese have two operational aircraft carriers derived from the Russian Kuzentsov-class and two more are under construction. (PLAN)

BELOW: The RFS *Admiral Kuznetsov* is currently undergoing a major refit and overhaul to enable it to serve for another decade. Plans for a new Russian super carrier appear to have been put on hold. (MOD/CROWN COPYRIGHT)

Future Naval Tech

Changing the Nature of Naval Warfare

> *"In a future scenario if we find ourselves unable to compete traditionally in terms of mass, we must think differently if we are to regain operational advantage."*
>
> Second Sea Lord, Vice Admiral Nick Hine, September 2021

ABOVE: Armed unmanned surface vessels are being lined up to replace rigid inflatable boats operated from Royal Navy frigates to protect them from swarms of enemy gun boats. (MOD/CROWN COPYRIGHT)

Naval warfare has always been dominated by a drive to achieve technological advantage. Steam power brought the age of sail to an end. Rifled artillery made the cannonball obsolete. Submarines and aircraft became the dominant naval weapons in World War One and Two. The advent of nuclear weapons turned submarines armed with nuclear-tipped ballistic missiles into the ultimate doomsday machines.

In the 21st century a new revolution in naval technology is underway as rapid advances take place in robotics and artificial intelligence, or AI. The prospect of removing human beings from large areas of naval activity has led many navies, including the Royal Navy, to take a hard look at how they design and build future warships.

For many decades there has been a growing trend in ship designs to increase the use of mechanical automation, and the Royal Navy has incorporated this technology in many of its warships. The new 65,000 ton Queen Elizabeth-class aircraft carriers, for example, make

RIGHT: Royal Navy control rooms are being transformed by advanced communications and Artificial Intelligence. (MOD/CROWN COPYRIGHT)

extensive use of lifts and ammunition handling technology to reduce its crew size to 679 (minus air group personnel) compared to the 650 on the 22,000 ton Invincible-class carriers they replaced. US Navy Nimitz-class carriers come in at 100,000 tons and have a ship's company of 3,500. So, the Royal Navy has dramatically automated many functions on its new

aircraft carriers to enable it to reduce their crew sizes.

Mechanical automation is only the first step in the Royal Navy's drive to incorporate new technology in its warships. Robotic technology is on the verge of being introduced across the fleet, starting with the mine countermeasures domain and air operations.

Robots mean human crews can be excluded from dangerous missions, they improve performance and allow more capability to be purchased for the same or less money.

AI offers the prospect of transforming naval warfare by dramatically speeding up the decision making. This is considered essential in an era of hypersonic missiles, where a naval task force's air defences could potentially

only be given a few seconds – rather than minutes, as is the case now – to react to in-bound missiles. These types of reaction times make it very difficult for real-life naval officers in ships' control rooms to understand what is happening and issue orders to activate defences or fire weapons to deal with hypersonic threats. AI-based defence systems could sift through thousands of radar contacts and other intelligence information and in a few seconds determine if they are real threats. Then the AI system could direct weapons to intercept and neutralise the threats, all in a matter of seconds.

This raises the issue about the degree to which a fleet's air defences should be automated and humans removed from the chain of command. Until now the Royal Navy – along with its NATO counterparts – have resisted allowing the employment of lethal force by robots. A 'human-in-the-loop' command remains central to all Royal Navy rules of engagement to prevent tragedies and ensure that responsibility for killing people lies with naval officers in all circumstances. If potential opponents adopt AI-based command systems and hypersonic weapons they could achieve such a decisive advantage that the Royal Navy and its allies could have no choice but to follow suit.

The first types of robots entering Royal Navy services are in the mine countermeasures role. The £25m ATLAS Remote Combined Influence Minesweeping System (ARCIMS) contract was awarded in early 2021 to Atlas Elektronik UK for the supply of three combined-influence minesweeping systems. The French Defence Procurement Agency (DGA) and UK MOD's Defence Equipment & Support (DE&S) organisations are working in co-operation with the European procurement organisation OCCAR to acquire the Maritime Mine Counter Measures (MMCM) capability for the Royal Navy and its French allies. These systems are in the process of being delivered.

In 2021 young engineers from UK Naval Engineering, Science & Technology (UKNEST) were set the challenge of proposing a Future Autonomous Fleet programme that could shape how the Royal Navy operates over the next 50 years.

In the future they envisage drones, or unmanned aerial vehicles, based »

ABOVE: Royal Navy fleet divers who have to inspect enemy sea mines could be replaced by unmanned underwater vehicles. (MOD/CROWN COPYRIGHT)

BELOW: Traditional air defence systems are potentially being rendered obsolete by hypersonic missiles. (BABCOCK)

ABOVE: Experiments with delivery drones are being conducted by 700X Naval Air Squadron, the Fleet Air Arm's new trials and testing unit. (MOD/CROWN COPYRIGHT)

BELOW: The Royal Navy's ice patrol ship HMS *Protector* has its own drones to monitor the environment in the Antarctic region. (MOD/CROWN COPYRIGHT)

in the stratosphere to be launched at a moment's notice, uncrewed fast-attack crafts housing smaller autonomous boats, aircraft carriers propelled by both sea-based biofuels and wind power, and an underwater flagship at the centre of the fleet. Other conceptual ideas include the increased use of Artificial Intelligence to assist with low-level planning and underwater transport units carrying anything from munitions to food.

While this futurist vision is a long-term road map for the Royal Navy, elements of it will take time to be realised. The Royal Navy has set up several groups to exploit and integrate new technology, including:

• Office of the Chief Technology Officer (OTCO), based at Navy Command Headquarters in Portsmouth, Hampshire. It is required 'to accelerate the embrace of all forms of technology across all areas of the Royal Navy'.

• NavyX is the Royal Navy's new Autonomy and Lethality Accelerator with a mandate to 'rapidly develop, test and trial cutting-edge equipment, with the aim of getting new technology off the drawing board and into the hands of our people on operations at a pace that has not been possible before. It will operate across all maritime environments – over water, on water, underwater and the littoral'. It has the biggest portfolio of all the Royal Navy science and technology projects.

• Discover, Analysis and Rapid Exploitation (DARE) team. The DARE team explores ways of providing cutting-edge technology and operational prototypes to show where the Royal Navy could go in the future.

• NEMESIS. This is the Royal Navy's autonomy and experimentation hub, which is working on higher level AI applications.

• MarWorks, which specialises in

delivering architectures to support tactical data flow and feeds over secure, agile communications. It is the Royal Navy's information warfare technology accelerator and collaborates with the user communities by conducting rapid experimentation to exploit leading technologies for the navy.

• NELSON, the Royal Navy's own internal software house that develops computer applications.

One of the first projects to emerge from the NavyX group has been the Persistent Operational Deployment Systems (PODS) initiative. PODS are interchangeable modules that can be fitted to the vessels of the surface fleet. Similar in design to a shipping container, the PODS create the idea of a 'plug and play' warship and will enable Royal Navy ships of all sizes to be more adaptable and versatile when deployed.

The PODS could be delivered using innovative technology, such as heavy-lift drones or autonomous boats, so a warship will be able to receive more quickly the equipment it needs in order to be re-tasked, without the need to go into a port to collect it.

Equipment to be housed in the PODS could include autonomous boats for surveillance and reconnaissance, mobile command centres, quadcopter drones to deliver supplies, humanitarian aid and disaster relief stores, and medical facilities.

Over the past four years the NavyX organisation has run several technology demonstrations of unmanned underwater vessels (UUVs) or unmanned surface vessels (USVs) that give an idea of the future systems that could enter Royal Navy service. They include:

• Maritime Demonstrator For Operational eXperimentation

(MADFOX), which is an autonomous vessel that could be used to conduct reconnaissance operations and surveillance patrols, providing valuable information on a coastal area before Royal Marines get in their raiding craft to come ashore.

• Raydrive. The Oxford-based Animal Dynamics provided NavyX with its Raydrive UUV, which is 1m by 1.25m in size and uses silent fish-like propulsion. This is aimed at trialling sensors and communications for use during covert intelligence, and reconnaissance missions.

• Manta Extra Large Unmanned Underwater Vehicle (XLUUV) is a demonstration project to build an underwater robot to operate at ranges out to 3,000 nautical miles. The first of two phases of this £2.5 million project was scheduled to be completed by April 2022. Phase 2 covers two years of mission testing of gradually increasing complexity.

• Project Hecla aims to refine future operating concepts of USVs in a military undersea-surveying application, using an Otter Pro catamaran USV developed by Maritime Robotics of Norway.

• Pacific 24 Rigid Inflatable Boat (RIB). This was a 12-month, £3.2 million contract with BAE Systems' Portsmouth-based Maritime Services covering the trialling of unmanned and armed Pacific 24 USVs in intelligence, surveillance, and force protection roles, as well as the integration of an unmanned RIB into the combat management system of a Type 23 frigate.

ABOVE: The MADFOX Autonomous Surface Vehicle is a test-bed vessel that is being used for trials with experimental weapons and sensors. (MOD/CROWN COPYRIGHT)

BELOW: Expendable mini drones are already revolutionising naval warfare. (US NAVY)

The Shipbuilding Programme

Rebuilding the Royal Navy

Over the next decade the Royal Navy is to spend more than £83bn on new ships, submarines, and other maritime equipment. And this does not include the cost of the Lockheed Martin F-35B Lightning II jump jets that are being bought to fly off the Queen Elizabeth-class aircraft carriers. Each F-35B costs around £100m and some 26 more are expected to be bought over the next decade, so that could add another £2.5bn to the Royal Navy's shopping bill.

Few navies in the world can boast an order book of similar size and it is a sign of the commitment of the British government to boost the country's maritime power. The 2021 Integrated Review of Britain's defence and security needs added £8bn of new spending to the shipbuilding plan.

Type 26/City Class
This is the most advanced element of the shipbuilding programme that got underway a decade ago to replace most of the old Type 23 frigates. Eight of the new frigates are on order as part of a £6bn contract with BAE Systems. The first ship, HMS *Glasgow*, is at an

CITY CLASS	
Name	Pennant Number
Batch 1	
HMS *Glasgow*	F88
HMS *Cardiff*	F89
HMS *Belfast*	F90
Batch 2	
HMS *Birmingham*	
HMS *Sheffield*	
HMS *Newcastle*	
HMS *Edinburgh*	
HMS *London*	

advanced stage of construction at the company's Govan yard in Scotland and is expected to be handed over to the Royal Navy for acceptance trials to begin in the middle of the decade. Frontline operational service is projected for 2027.

These ships are designed as general-purpose warships and in Royal Navy service they will be optimised for anti-submarine warfare. They are built around a mission-bay concept, which is designed to allow containers fitted with mission-specific equipment, such as unmanned aerial vehicle launch and control facilities or medical facilities, to be rapidly moved onboard and brought into use.

The Royal Navy and BAE Systems created the vessel with export potential in mind, and so it is also known as the Global Combat Ship. Australia and Canada have since adopted the design, and it is known

in the Royal Australian Navy as the Hunter Class. It is also known as the Canadian Surface Combatant.

Type 31/Inspiration Class

This class of frigate is intended to be a 'low end' or 'constabulary' warship. Babcock International's Arrowhead 140 design was selected in September 2019 and two months later the company went on contract.

The ships are being constructed at Babcock's Rosyth shipyard in Fife after the keel of the first ship was laid in April 2022.

Five ships are already under the contract and first of class is due to

INSPIRATION CLASS
HMS *Venturer*
HMS *Bulldog*
HMS *Campbeltown*
HMS *Formidable*
HMS *Active*

enter service in 2027 to replace retiring Type 23s. Unlike the Type 23s, the new ships will not be optimised for anti-submarine operations. They are to have mission bays to allow unmanned system and mine countermeasures equipment to be rapidly installed. »

ABOVE: Babcock has built a dedicated frigate assembly hall at its Rosyth shipyard to build the Type 32 ships for the Royal Navy and export customers. (BABCOCK)

BELOW: Babcock's Arrowhead 140 design, which derived from the Danish Navy's Iver Huitfeldt Class, won the competition to be the Type 31 Inspiration-class frigate for the Royal Navy. (BABCOCK)

Type 32

A further five 'low end' frigates were confirmed in the 2021 Integrated Review of defence and security. They were initially talked of as Type 31 batch 2 warships, but the Ministry of Defence now says a concept phase study is underway to determine what it actually wants. When in service after 2030 they will boost Royal Navy destroyer and frigate numbers to 24 units.

Type 83 Future Maritime Air Defence Platform

This is intended to replace the Type 45 destroyers in the 2030s. The project was launched by the 2021 Integrated Review and is at an early stage.

Fleet Solid Support Ships

This £2bn programme is intended to replace the Fort-class support ships of the Royal Fleet Auxiliary (RFA) but it has been delayed for several years over arguments about where the vessels will be built. Ministry of Defence officials initially proposed that foreign shipyards should be allowed to bid to build the ships, sparking outrage among ministers and politicians.

The competition is now underway after minsters insisted that the consortium building the ships had to be British led. The first ship will have to be in service by 2028 and the last

one is to be delivered by 2032. RFA *Fort Victoria* may have to be extended in service to ensure a solid support vessel is available to support the Queen Elizabeth-class carriers.

Multi-Role Support Ship
The Royal Navy envisages replacing the Albion-class dock and Bay-class landing ships with a common family of ships, as well as the RFA *Argus* which provides both aviation training support and can be converted into a hospital ship.

The new ships are due to enter service in the 2030s but studies to define requirements have still not been completed.

Multi-Role Ocean Surveillance Ship
This new type of ship is needed to protect underwater communications from sabotage or espionage. The vessels are intended to deploy unmanned underwater vehicles and advanced sonar arrays to monitor suspicious activity near underwater cables.

The Ministry of Defence originally proposed having the first vessel ready for service by mid-decade but it has yet to begin the contracting process.

Dreadnought SSBN
The replacement of the Vanguard-class submarines is the largest UK defence procurement project of the decade and is expected to cost in excess of £30bn. Construction of the submarines has begun at BAE Systems' yard in Barrow-in-Furness and the first boat is expected to enter service soon after 2030, although the exact date is considered top secret by the Ministry of Defence.

The new submarines will fire the Lockheed Martin Trident II D5 missiles, which are also used by

the current Vanguard boats. The Dreadnought project includes the building of new reactor cores and the renewal of Britain's nuclear warheads. BAE Systems' Devonshire Dock Hall assembly building is being modernised to accommodate the new submarines. The Royal Navy's Faslane submarine base on the Clyde in Glasgow is also to be modernised for their arrival.

Maritime Underwater Future Capability
Work has already started on a project to design and build a successor to the Astute-class nuclear-powered attack submarines. The project, dubbed the Maritime Underwater Future Capability, is also known as Submersible Ship Nuclear (Replacement) or SSN(R). In September 2021, BAE Systems

and Rolls-Royce received contracts totalling £170m to start work on the new submarine that is intended to enter service after 2040.

National Flagship
This controversial project was first talked about as a replacement for the long-retired HMRY *Britannia*, but according to media reports, before her death HM The Queen let it be known that she did not want to be associated with the ship. Former Prime Minister Boris Johnson then said the vessel would be used to showcase the best of British industry. Tender documents released by the Ministry of Defence in 2021 said the ship would cost between £200m and £250m to build. The demise of Johnson's premiership on September 5, 2022, has led to suggestions the project will be dropped.

ABOVE: The £30bn project to build the new Dreadnought Class of ballistic missile submarines to replace the existing Vanguard-class submarines is Britain's most expensive-ever defence project. (BAE SYSTEMS)

BELOW: Work on the new HMS *Glasgow* is well advanced at BAE Systems' Govan shipyard on the Clyde in Glasgow. (BAE SYSTEMS)

Future of the Royal Navy

British Naval Power in 21st Century

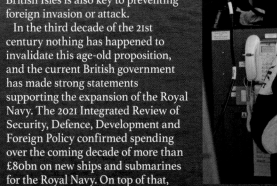

ABOVE: The new Type 26 frigates have purpose-designed multi-mission bays to allow new systems such as aerial or underwater drones to be rapidly deployed onto the ship. (BAE SYSTEMS)

RIGHT: Incorporating Artificial Intelligence in warships' control rooms is driving an intense debate over the role of humans in authorising the employment of lethal force. (MOD/CROWN COPYRIGHT)

As an island nation Britain has long sought to be a naval power because its prosperity is dependent on securing global sea lanes to ensure trade continues to flow freely. Command of the seas around the British Isles is also key to preventing foreign invasion or attack.

In the third decade of the 21st century nothing has happened to invalidate this age-old proposition, and the current British government has made strong statements supporting the expansion of the Royal Navy. The 2021 Integrated Review of Security, Defence, Development and Foreign Policy confirmed spending over the coming decade of more than £80bn on new ships and submarines for the Royal Navy. On top of that,

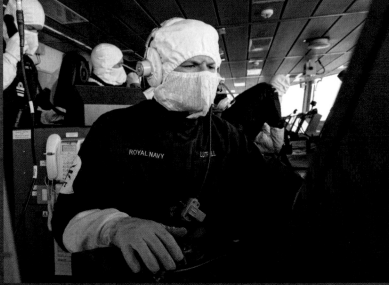

in 2021-22 alone, £7.5bn was spent on running the Royal Navy, paying salaries, providing fuel, food and ammunition for ships, as well as overhauling warships. If this spending is maintained, then Britain is on track to spend at least £155bn on naval power up to 2032. Never in its history has the Royal Navy been so well

resourced and it would suggest it has a secure future.

Bringing the New Fleet on Line

We have laid out earlier in this edition of the *Royal Navy Yearbook* the ambitious plans to modernise the fleet with new ships, submarines,

and aircraft, as well as weapons and equipment for the Royal Marines.

The new hardware is not going to arrive all at once and the Royal Navy is going to have to manage a transition to the new equipment, while keeping its existing vessels fully operational.

Looking at the delivery schedules of the new vessels »

ABOVE: The Type 31 Inspiration-class frigates are designed to operate in so-called 'low end' environments where full combat capabilities are not required. (BABCOCK)

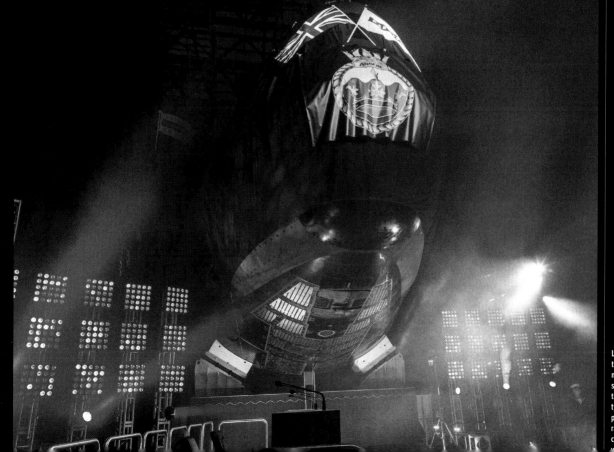

LEFT: HMS *Anson* and the other Astute-class nuclear power attack submarines could be the last vessels of this type that the Royal Navy purchases as it looks to radically recast how it conducts underwater warfare. (BAE SYSTEMS)

ABOVE: Radical new construction techniques are needed to reduce the cost of future warships and allow the Royal Navy to maintain its hull numbers in an era of rapid cost inflation. (BAE SYSTEMS)

BELOW: Experiments with unmanned aerial vehicles are underway in many navies in strike, reconnaissance, rescue, and cargo delivery roles. (HANS FREDRIK)

and submarines, it is clear the Royal Navy is focusing on specific capabilities in a rolling programme of investment. Up to 2025 the priority is being given to spending on the delivery of the final three Astute attack submarines and bringing the carrier strike capability fully on line by taking delivery of the first tranche of 48 Lockheed Martin F-35B Lightning combat aircraft.

After 2025 spending on the Royal Navy's new frigates – the Type 26s and Type 31s – will start to ramp up as these new ships begin to be delivered in quantity. This will also be the period of peak spending on the Dreadnought programme to replace the Vanguard Class of ballistic missile-firing submarines ahead of entry to service of the new HMS *Vanguard* around 2030. Billions of pounds are also to be spent on new infrastructure at Faslane naval base, including futuristic simulators to train the crews of the new submarines.

In the early years of the 2030s, spending on the remaining three Dreadnought boats will continue to run high and the new Type 32 frigates will also come on line to expand the size of the surface fleet. The Albion- and Bay-class amphibious ships are scheduled to be replaced in this period with the new Multi-Role Support Ships (MRSS). It is also envisaged that a whole new mine countermeasures force will enter service at that time, using predominately autonomous systems.

Towards the end of the 2030s will be the time to focus attention on replacing the Type 45 destroyers and the early boats of the Astute Class.

As the Royal Navy enters the 2040s it will boast a fleet of warships and submarines that will mostly be fewer than 20 years old, and this should set it on a steady course into the latter half of the century.

How will New Tech Change the Royal Navy?

Laying out the Royal Navy's plans to build new ships and submarines is only half of the picture. The weapons, sensors and supporting systems that are installed on its vessels are perhaps just as important as the hulls.

One of the most significant new areas of interest for the Royal Navy is the fielding of hypersonic missiles. These threaten to render existing air defence systems obsolete and a navy that can bring them into service in significant numbers could secure a decisive advantage. Russian forces employed hypersonic weapons for the first time in the war against Ukraine early in 2022, so there is real pressure on the Royal Navy to acquire those weapons.

First Sea Lord, Admiral Sir Ben Key, told an audience of industrialists at Rosyth dockyard in February 2022: *"It's a future where we are setting ourselves a challenge to become a global leader in hypersonic weapons."*

In April 2022, the leaders of Britain, Australia and the United States committed to launching a joint effort to developing and fielding hypersonic weapons.

In tandem with developing these offensive hypersonic weapons, the Royal Navy is looking to improve the effectiveness of its air defences by incorporating advanced Artificial Intelligence programmes and algorithms in its radar networks and command systems. It is hoped that this technology will dramatically increase the ability of radars to detect targets, analyse the threats they pose and allow the rapid activation of defensive weapons.

Traditional guns and missiles might not be enough to counter the airborne threats of tomorrow and, in September 2021, the Ministry of Defence contracted Thales UK in Belfast to provide a maritime laser-directed energy weapon, or LDEW, for a Type 23 frigate. Known as Project Tracey, this capability demonstrator weapon will be installed on a Type 23 frigate for user-experimentation trials starting in 2023, with the system integrated into the ship's combat system for the duration. Experiments will explore the full decision-making process for engaging threats, and will include detecting, tracking, engaging and countering UAVs as well as sea targets. According to the MOD, the design requirements are focused on providing user experience. The intention is to allow the Royal Navy to de-risk the operation of high-energy lasers in realistic environments. The team on Project Tracey is led by Thales UK and also includes BAE Systems, Chess Dynamics, Vision4ce and IPG.

The Royal Navy is also on the cusp of bringing into service its first fully autonomous mine countermeasure systems. These allow traditionally crewed mine countermeasure vessels to be replaced by unmanned vessels and underwater vehicles. Mine clearing has long been a dangerous business and replacing humans with robots makes a lot of sense, as well as saving the Royal Navy a lot of money. The future mine clearing equipment will be operated from portable mission modules that can be mounted on a variety of vessels. The new Type 26 and 31 frigates, for example, have mission bays incorporated in their designs to allow the specialist mission modules to be installed depending on their task. The mine clearing modules could also be carried by amphibious vessels or the future Multi-Role Support Ships.

Unmanned surface vessels are also being trialled by the Royal Navy and Royal Marines to take over many of the tasks currently conducted by fast patrol boats. Again, the mission bays of the future frigates could be used to launch armed raiding craft to take on swarms of enemy fast-attack craft or carry out covert reconnaissance missions close to enemy-held shorelines.

The Royal Navy has contracted to build an experimental robot submarine with a 3,000 nautical mile range and three-month endurance. Work started in 2020 on an initial prototype, dubbed the Extra Large Uncrewed Underwater Vehicle (XLUUX), or Manta. This is a potentially revolutionary weapon system that could upend all previous ways of conducting underwater operations.

Land-based unmanned aerial vehicles have made a major impact on warfare over the past two decades, but sea-based drones are still catching up. The Royal Navy is »

BELOW: Royal Marine raiding forces are experimenting with armed unmanned surface vessels. (MOD/CROWN COPYRIGHT)

ABOVE: The Future Commando Force is trialling drones, advanced communications, lightweight materials and miniature weapons to improve the capability of the Royal Marines.
(MOD/CROWN COPYRIGHT)

experimenting with mini drones that can be launched from small craft for close surveillance. Large drones with longer endurance and jet engines are soon to be test launched from HMS *Prince of Wales*. In the longer term, the Royal Navy is looking to replace their Merlin Crowsnest airborne early warning helicopters with a long-endurance drone.

Building the Fleet After Next

The former US Defense Secretary, Donald Rumsfeld, once famously talked about "known unknowns" complicating future defence planning. This could be also translated as 'prepare for the unknown'.

For the Royal Navy, the rapid advances taking place in many areas of defence technology – hypersonic weapons, AI, and robot craft – make it exceedingly difficult to plan how it will function in future operational environments. Perhaps the best way to prepare for an era of continuous change is to remain flexible and keep all options open.

In 2021, the Royal Navy unveiled its Future Fleet concept for the 2050s, which envisaged an array of futuristic vessels. The need to hide from satellite surveillance and swarms of aerial drones has prompted

the designers of this concept to dramatically increase the use of submarines to host fleet flagships and move troops and supplies as well as amphibious forces. Only uncrewed vessels would be risked in surface operations close to enemy shores or within range of their airpower and land-based missiles. To help counter the climate crisis, increasing use is being made of nuclear power, biofuels, and solar power. Although not quite a return to the golden age of sail, future warships will have to find alternative ways of generating power other than burning diesel.

Work on the fleet of the 2050s has not yet begun but Royal Navy experts and the British ship building industry are already working on ships for the 2040s. The Type 83 Future Maritime Air Defence Platform and the Maritime Underwater Future Capability or Submersible Ship Nuclear (Replacement) [SSN(R)] are both on computer-aided design screens in a number of shipyards and research centres. The early work suggests that it would be wrong to describe these as either new destroyers or new attack submarines. The Type 83 is envisaged as hosting a powerful battery of anti-aircraft missiles, but it is also likely to boast an array of

long-range land-attack missiles and be capable of launching drones with powerful airborne early warning radars. High level automation in every aspect will also mean cutting the number of crew required to man a Type 45 from the current 191 to around 50.

When it comes to the SSN(R), even more radical ideas are being considered. If the Manta robot submarine experiment proves a success, then the SSN(R) could be the launch platform, or mother ship, for a whole family of unmanned underwater vehicles, including ocean floor survey drones and coastal surveillance and attack variants. The new submarine could be the control hub for swarms of drones, which in theory could dominate huge swathes of ocean, both above and below the surface.

Swarms of robot drones appears a long way from the days of Horatio Nelson directing a fleet of sailing ships and firing iron broadsides at wooden-hulled enemy vessels a few hundred yards away. However, despite the rush to field autonomous intelligence and other robot systems, it seems certain that the Royal Navy will still need human sailors to direct, control and repair these mechanical warriors.

LEFT: Royal Navy officers in the 21st century will face an array of operational and tactical challenges that few can imagine today. (MOD/CROWN COPYRIGHT)

BELOW: An improvised submarine operated by drug smugglers is intercepted by US Navy vessels, illustrating that advanced technology is rapidly proliferating around the world. (US NAVY)

Royal Navy Glossary

AEW: Airborne Early Warning

ASuW: Anti-surface Warfare

ASW: Anti-submarine Warfare

CGRM: Commandant General Royal Marines

COD: Carrier Onboard Delivery

COMATG: Commander Amphibious Task Group

CSAR: Combat Search and Rescue

CSG: Carrier Strike Group

CV: Aircraft Carrier

CVN: Aircraft Carrier, nuclear powered

CWIS: Close-in Weapon System

Det: Detachment

EU: European Union

FCF: Future Commando Force

FOST: Flag Officer Sea Training

FS: French Ship

GPMG: General Purpose Machine Gun

HMAS: His Majesty's Australian Ship

HMNB: His Majesty's Naval Base

HMS: His Majesty's Ship

JMSDF: Japanese Maritime Self Defense Force

JPR: Joint Personnel Recovery

LCU: Landing Craft Utility

LCVP: Landing Craft Vehicle Personnel

LHA: Landing Helicopter Assault ship

LIFEX: Life Extension upgrade and maintenance

LPD: Landing Platform Dock ship

LPH: Landing Platform Helicopter ship

LSD: Landing Ship Dock

LSG: Littoral Strike Group

LSS: Littoral Strike Ship

MCM: Mine Countermeasures

MEU (SOC): Marine Expeditionary Unit (Special Operations Capable) (USMC)

NATO: North Atlantic Treaty Organisation

NAS: Naval Air Squadron

NRF: NATO Response Force

PLAN: People's Liberation Army Navy

PLANS: People's Liberation Army Navy Ship

RAF: Royal Air Force

RAN: Royal Australian Navy

RFS: Russian Federation Ship

RIB: Rigid Inflatable Boat

RFA: Royal Fleet Auxiliary

RM: Royal Marines

RN: Royal Navy

TAG: Tailored Air Group

TF: Task Force

TLAM: Tomahawk Land Attack Missile

UAV: Unmanned Aerial Vehicle

UN: United Nations

USMC: US Marine Corps

USN: US Navy

USS: United States Ship

USV: Unmanned Surface Vehicle

UUV: Unmanned Underwater Vehicle

ABOVE: HMS *Queen Elizabeth* and HMS *Prince of Wales* sail side by side in a rare meeting at sea. (MOD/CROWN COPYRIGHT)